BASICS
PHOTOGRAPHY
01

COMPOSITION

David Prakel

Ethical: aware-
ness/
reflect-
ion/
debate

An AVA Book

Published by AVA Publishing SA
Rue des Fontenailles 16
Case Postale
1000 Lausanne 6
Switzerland
Tel: +41 786 005 109
Email: enquiries@avabooks.ch

Distributed by Thames & Hudson (ex-North America)
181a High Holborn
London WC1V 7QX
United Kingdom
Tel: +44 20 7845 5000
Fax: +44 20 7845 5055
Email: sales@thameshudson.co.uk
www.thamesandhudson.com

Distributed in the USA and Canada by:
Ingram Publisher Services Inc.
1 Ingram Blvd.
La Vergne TN 37086
USA
Tel: +1 866 400 5351
Fax: +1 800 838 1149
Email: customer.service@ingrampublisherservices.com

English Language Support Office
AVA Publishing (UK) Ltd.
Tel: +44 1903 204 455
Email: enquiries@avabooks.ch

ISBN 978-2-940373-04-8

10 9 8 7 6

Design by Gavin Ambrose (www.gavinambrose.co.uk)

Production by AVA Book Production Pte. Ltd., Singapore
Tel: +65 6334 8173
Fax: +65 6259 9830
Email: production@avabooks.com.sg

All reasonable attempts have been made to trace, clear and credit the
copyright holders of the images reproduced in this book. However, if any
credits have been inadvertently omitted, the publisher will endeavour to
incorporate amendments in future editions.

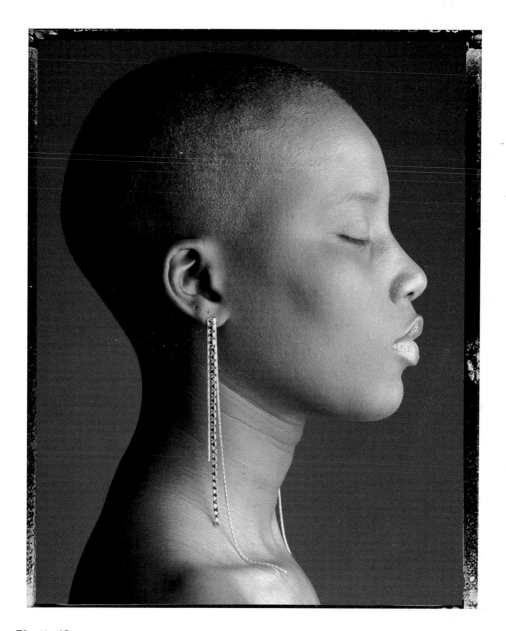

Binette 12

This portrait by Nana Sousa Dias is composed very simply to emphasise the beautiful, bold, graphic shape, texture and lighting of the subject's features.

Photographer: Nana Sousa Dias.

Technical summary: Pentax 645 with Pentax 135mm macro lens, 1/60 sec at f22, Ilford HP5 Plus, lit by Multiblitz Magnolite 32 flash-head with 1m square softbox.

Contents ▷

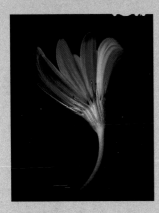
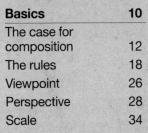
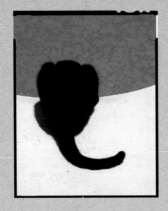
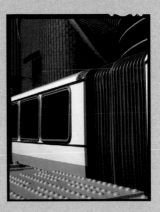

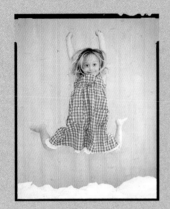
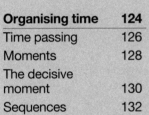
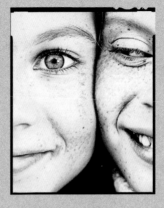
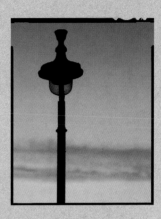

This book features dedicated chapters explaining the process of composition, its formal elements and how space and time are organised in photographic images. It is illustrated throughout with classic images from the masters of photography, and creative images – some taken especially for this book – from contemporary practitioners. Later chapters look at how techniques of composition can be applied in real-world situations and used to create a personal style. Each key idea is isolated, examined and explained in context.

Main chapter pages

These offer a précis of the basic concepts that will be discussed

Headings

Each important concept is shown in the heading at the top of each spread to enable readers to refer quickly to a topic of interest.

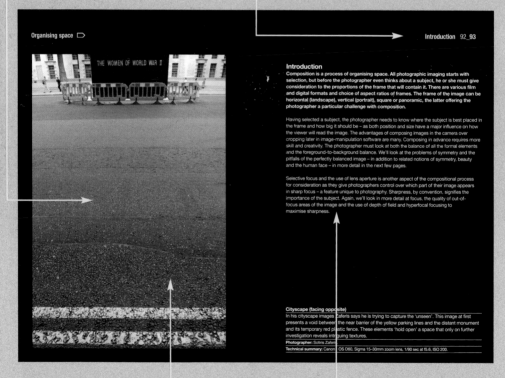

Organising space ▷

Introduction 92_93

Introduction

Composition is a process of organising space. All photographic imaging starts with selection, but before the photographer even thinks about a subject, he or she must give consideration to the proportions of the frame that will contain it. There are various film and digital formats and choice of aspect ratios of frames. The frame of the image can be horizontal (landscape), vertical (portrait), square or panoramic, the latter offering the photographer a particular challenge with composition.

Having selected a subject, the photographer needs to know where the subject is best placed in the frame and how big it should be – as both position and size have a major influence on how the viewer will read the image. The advantages of composing images in the camera over cropping later in image-manipulation software are many. Composing in advance requires more skill and creativity. The photographer must look at both the balance of all the formal elements and the foreground-to-background balance. We'll look at the problems of symmetry and the pitfalls of the perfectly balanced image – in addition to related notions of symmetry, beauty and the human face – in more detail in the next few pages.

Selective focus and the use of lens aperture is another aspect of the compositional process for consideration as they give photographers control over which part of their image appears in sharp focus – a feature unique to photography. Sharpness, by convention, signifies the importance of the subject. Again, we'll look in more detail at focus, the quality of out-of-focus areas of the image and the use of depth of field and hyperfocal focusing to maximise sharpness.

Cityscape (facing opposite)

In his cityscape images Zaferis says he is trying to capture the 'unseen'. This image at first presents a void between the near barrier of the yellow parking lines and the distant monument and its temporary red plastic fence. These elements 'hold open' a space that only on further investigation reveals intriguing textures.

Photographer: Sotiris Zaferis

Technical summary: Canon EOS D60, Sigma 15–30mm zoom lens, 1/90 sec at f5.6, ISO 200.

Introductory images

Introductory images give a visual indication of the context for each chapter.

Introductions

Special section introductions outline basic concepts that will be discussed.

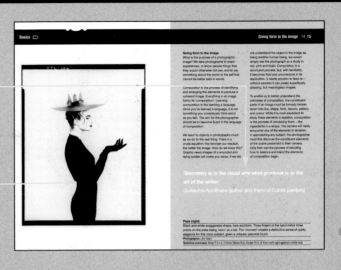

Quotations

The pertinent thoughts
and comments of famous
photographers, artists and
photographic commentators.

Images

All the images have been carefully
chosen to illustrate the principles
under discussion.

Image captions

Captions call attention to particular
facets of composition and often list the
technical equipment used and
exposure details.

Diagrams

Diagrams explain technical and
compositional concepts clearly
and concisely.

Introduction ▷

The best images combine technical excellence and strong composition. Though not everyone would agree about the processes of photographic composition, all would agree that an image is stronger for its application. Photographic technique may be complex, but its application is methodical and the outcome predictable. Composition, in contrast, requires discrimination and the application of personal taste. It is a difficult subject, especially for those beginning to explore photography as a profession or art form. Many photographers initially look for a checklist or book of rules that matches the predictability of photographic technique.

The first rule of composition is there are no rules. While photographic technique can be taken as a series of points for consideration or action in turn (choice of film and format, focusing, exposure, etc.) it is not possible to do this with composition. The method of composing, in other words, putting together a powerful image, cannot be a checklist approach but must be holistic. One key to understanding is that the eye and the camera 'see' things quite differently. This book examines how an appreciation of this can be used to develop photographic seeing.

The role of composition is better explained by way of analogy with the world of music. Photography should be like jazz – an improvisatory form of music where personal expression is everything but that expression is based on a solid structure of learned chords and chord progression. When we talk, we do not consciously consider the grammar of our language; in the same way, we need to practise composition until it becomes second nature. We can do this by experimenting with the isolated formal elements and by looking at the widest possible range of well-composed images. This book is meant to kick-start these processes.

Basics

For a viewer to make sense of an image it must be well composed. This section looks at that need for organisation and at ideas from fine art that have dominated photographic thinking in the past.

Formal elements

If composition is the underlying grammar of a visual language, then the formal elements – simple line, shapes, tone, form, textures, patterns and colour – are its vocabulary.

Organising space

Creating a photographic image is to put a frame around a chosen subject. The proportions of the frame and where the subject is placed within it have important influences on how the image is 'read'. The photograph's unique ability to manipulate the appearance of space is examined.

Organising time

By definition, still photography captures the moving world in a static image. The photographer has the choice of smearing passing time or freezing the action. Choosing the peak moment to fire the shutter and image sequencing are explored.

Application

Major forms of photography involve different approaches to composition. This section makes suggestions for fine art, landscape, the nude and portraiture as well as for news, advertising and sports photography, where composition may not be considered a central contributing factor.

Originality

Putting over your own vision is important. This section discusses ways to develop a personal photographic style and how 'breaking the rules' can produce powerful images.

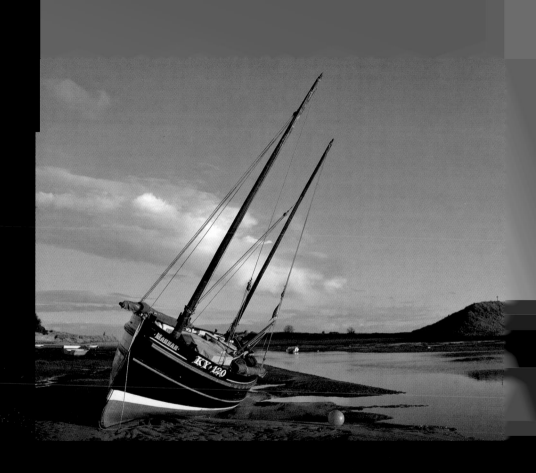

Alnmouth, Northumberland
This image represents the best-composed shot from a sequence taken at the same time

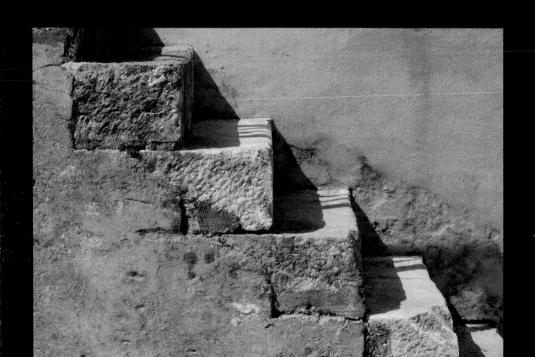

Composition has been a major concern for the photographic practitioner since the earliest days of photography in the mid-nineteenth century. Ideas from the world of fine art, based on an established history of art criticism, initially and completely overshadowed the fledgling craft. Many of the principles of painterly composition were forced upon photography. Devotees of the pictorial photographic movement embraced this move towards what they perceived to be the legitimisation of photography as an art form by the art establishment. However, more adventurous practitioners appreciated photography as a unique medium in its own right and rebelled against the conventions of fine-art composition.

Today, photography is democratised in a way that art never has been. Everyone can be a photographer. The history of the 'snapshot' is as long as the history of modern photography itself, most taken by enthusiasts with little formal appreciation of the rules of composition. In postmodern fashion, the casual snapshot has been appropriated by photographers and photographic artists who have knowingly hi-jacked it for creative ends. The sheer ubiquity of the photographic image in news media, advertising and commerce boldly casts aside historic notions of fine art, creating opportunities for new kinds of composition, though rather more stylised than before.

The rules of composition give photographers an organising principle and strength, but they can also be an artistic straitjacket, inhibiting creativity, and can lead to stereotypical images. Many of the so-called 'rules' of composition are based on an analysis of what the establishment and practitioners alike have traditionally considered to be effective images rather than on scientific experiment or survey.

This chapter looks at motivation and the psychology of photography and investigates the difference between a snapshot and a formally composed image. It also looks at some of the fine-art concepts that continue to be applied to photography and discusses which are and which aren't relevant.

Just stairs (facing opposite)

Estima's shot of a flight of stone stairs is another fine example of 'simplicity is best'. It is organised around a strong, symmetrically placed diagonal line – made by the repeating forms of the steps and shadows, which splits the composition into two planes. The image explores texture and the subtleties of a limited palette of colours as well as interesting variations in a repeating pattern.

Photographer: Tiago Estima.

Technical summary: Nikon D100 with 70–300mm Zoom-Nikkor, 1/180sec at f4.8, 180mm focal length.

The case for composition

The eye and the camera do not see the same things. The brain is actively, constantly processing information received from the eyes. It cuts out the unwanted detail that, in the camera's passive view, is given equal prominence.

Consider how many pictures are taken. Someone is carrying a camera. The fact they are carrying a camera means they intend to create images of some sort. What catches their eye depends entirely on their motivation for carrying the camera – their interest in people, landscape, wildlife, etc. When something catches their attention, they stop and bring the camera up to eye level. The shutter is released at the moment they 'see' what made them stop in the first place. Sometimes they press the shutter when their emotions peak. The images, when reviewed, are often never printed and nowadays remain abandoned on a computer hard-drive. If the images are printed and shown to others, an explanation of the events that were meant to be depicted usually accompanies them, along the lines of, 'You had to be there.'

What goes wrong is that the camera is being used to record the un-recordable. The shutter is released in an effort to capture a composite thought or personal reflection of a scene or event. The image, in other words, has not been composed. Constituent parts that identify and meaningfully bring together for the viewer the message of the image have somehow not been captured, leaving the meaning of the image unclear. We'll return to these constituent parts in the section on Formal elements on page 36.

One of the fundamental lessons in photography is to learn to photograph what you see, not what you think you see – it is too easy to make a photograph that coincides with your frame of mind at the time you pressed the shutter and not with what was actually in front of the camera lens.

Boy sailor (right)

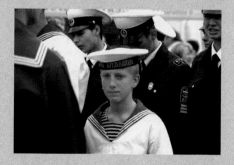

Snapshot. The young Russian naval cadet centred in the frame is not sufficiently differentiated from the other sailors. There are several distracting elements: white shapes in the background, the shoulder of the foreground sailor, the faces in the top right-hand corner of the frame and the sailor's face cut into the cadet's cap.

Photographer: David Präkel.

Technical summary: Nikon D100 with 70–300mm Zoom-Nikkor, 1/250sec at f4.2, 100mm focal length.

'There is a vast difference between taking a picture and making a photograph.' Robert Heinecken (photographer)

Boy sailor (below)

Composed and considered. A slight shift of viewpoint to the right and the use of zoom enabled the image to be cropped in-camera to cut out distracting faces from the rank of sailors in the background. Shutter speed was sacrificed for aperture to restore depth of field lost by an increase in focal length from 100 to 180mm, but fast enough to catch the boy's expression as he listens intently to the commanding officer's orders.

Photographer: David Präkel.

Technical summary: Nikon D100 with 70–300mm Zoom-Nikkor, 1/180sec at f4.8, 180mm focal length.

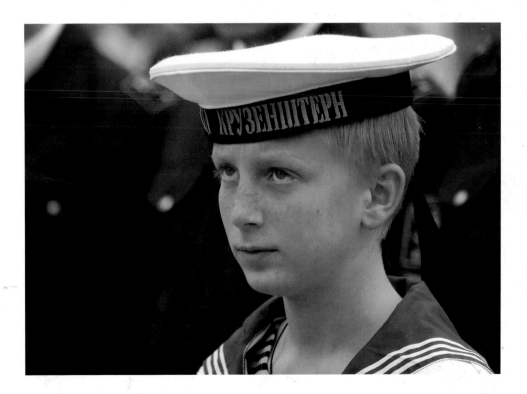

'What you see in the photograph isn't what you saw at the time. The real skill of photography is organised visual lying.' Terence Donovan (photographer)

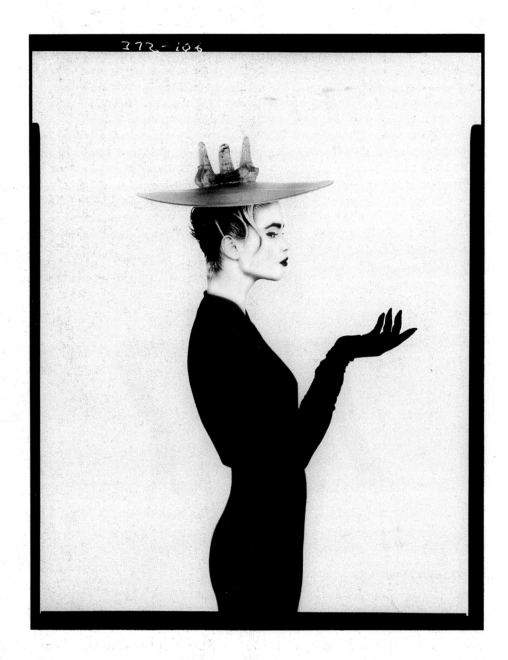

Giving form to the image

What is the purpose of a photographic image? We take photographs to share experiences, to show people things that they would otherwise not see, and to say something about the world or the self that cannot be better said in words.

Composition is the process of identifying and arranging the elements to produce a coherent image. Everything in an image forms its 'composition'. Learning composition is like learning a language. Once you've learned a language, it is not something you consciously think about as you talk. The aim for the photographer should be to become fluent in the language of composition.

We react to objects in photographs much as we do to the real thing. There is a crude equation: the stronger our reaction, the better the image. How do we know this? Graphic news images of a wounded and dying soldier will make you wince. If we did not understand the object in the image as being another human being, we would simply see the photograph as a study in red, pink and khaki. Composition is a structured process, but, with familiarity, it becomes fluid and unconscious in its application. It needs emotion to feed on – without emotion it can create superficially pleasing, but meaningless images.

To enable us to better understand the principles of composition, the constituent parts of an image must be formally broken down into line, shape, form, texture, pattern, and colour. While it is most expedient to study these elements in isolation, composition is the process of combining them – like ingredients in a recipe. The camera will rarely encounter one of the elements in isolation. In approaching any subject, the photographer must first discover the constituent elements of the scene presented to their camera. Only then can the process of deciding how to balance and blend the elements of composition begin.

'Geometry is to the visual arts what grammar is to the art of the writer.'
Guillaume Apollinaire (author and friend of Cubist painters)

Plate (facing opposite)

Black and white exaggerates shape, tone and form. Three fingers of the hand mirror three points on the plate being 'worn' as a hat. The 'moment' creates a distinctive sense of quirky elegance for this class subject, given a uniquely personal touch.

Photographer: Jim Allen.

Technical summary: Sinar P 5 x 4, 210mm Nikkor f5.6, Kodak Tri-X, lit from north light against a white wall.

'Photography is not about the thing photographed.
It is about how that thing looks photographed.'
Garry Winogrand (photographer)

Selection and arrangement
Drawing, painting and the process of taking a photograph have certain things in common. Each attempts to call a halt to the living world and to frame it in two dimensions.

The world is a dynamic, ever-changing place where people and objects move in three dimensions. In contrast, our photographs and paintings not only 'stop the clock' by their static nature, but also draw the viewer's attention to one framed part of the world, where the spatial relationships are now frozen into a very specific two-dimensional representation. In both painting and photography, dynamic becomes static and the three-dimensional world becomes flattened into two.

The artist constructs, works and reworks his or her image within its frame – referring back to the real world, maybe working with pure imagination. There is always the possibility of revision or change. In contrast, the photographer picks out a framed selection from the real world and organises the subject material within that frame.

Alternative photographic processes and digital manipulation provide some degree of image reworking, but the raw material of the photographic image comes from a selection made from the real world.

At first, photographers are tempted to put as much 'subject' as possible into their images, but, with experience, a better, more satisfying approach is to consciously edit the scene, considering what can be left out to simplify and strengthen the message. (Moving in closer is usually the best advice.) You know you have succeeded when you can look at an image in retrospect and see that all the elements have a specific function. When a photographer first becomes aware of the benefits of structuring an image as an aid to imparting a message he or she will begin consciously to select, frame and arrange. With practice, this will become second nature. Technical mastery is as important as composition, because the strongest message can only be revealed via a combination of strong composition and skilful photographic technique.

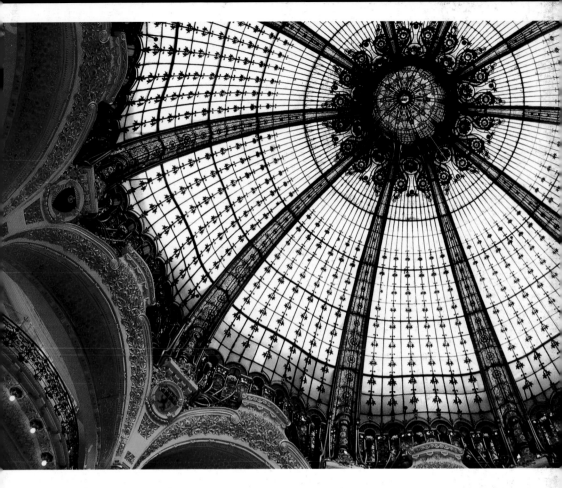

Galeries Lafayette (above)

From the riot of potential colourful subject matter in the newly refurbished Galeries Lafayette Haussmann store in Paris, the photographer judiciously selects the shape and pattern of the glass dome in the frame to include some the rich colours and contrasting scalloped shapes of the arcade.

Photographer: Bjorn Rannestad.

Technical summary: Sony DSC-V1, 1/80 sec at f2.8, ISO 100.

'It takes a lot of imagination to be a good photographer. You need less imagination to be a painter, because you can invent things.' David Bailey (photographer)

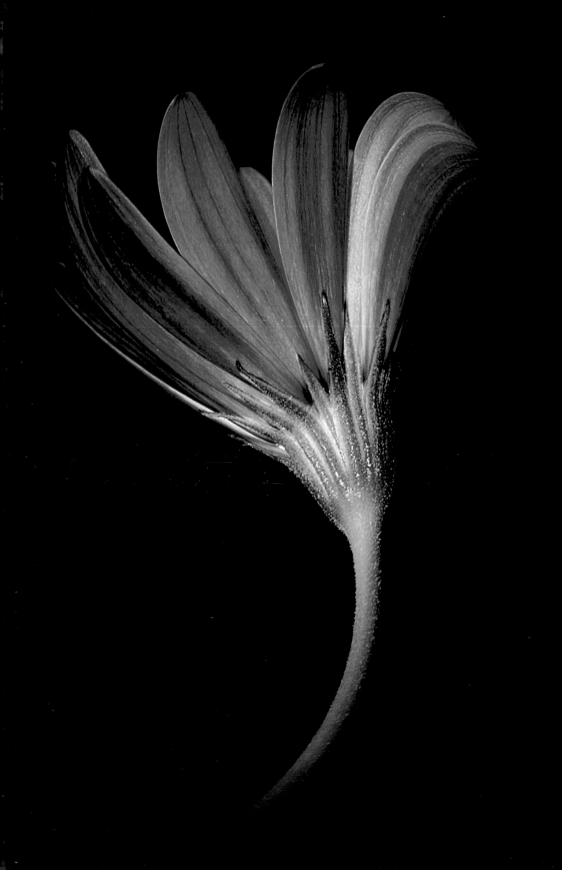

The rules

In the past, photographers often borrowed ideas from the fine arts and laboured with rules of composition that were, for them, only of use after the fact as a tool to analyse the finished image rather than to create it.

Painting and drawing are a synthesis of what has already been seen, expressed on canvas or paper. Even when working from life the artist can include items from his or her imagination and can edit out details or whole sections of the scene, something the photographer can only do to a limited extent. A photographer cannot simply decide not to photograph something that is already in the frame. Painting and drawing are the arts of constructing an image, but photography is the art of selection. Classical artists would strive to achieve harmony, balance and a beauty that transcends the real world. Photography so often *is* the real world.

The artist is free to rearrange the proportions and elements of the scene while painting so that they fall harmoniously on the canvas. Precise geometry can be used to place key components. Much of this process comes from an awareness of classical proportion and the embedding of basic shapes, triangles and circles into the composition.

To cover a canvas randomly with a range of coloured paints would take many times longer than it does to take a photograph. Most artists work their paintings for many hours and the images will evolve during this process. For the photographer, the moment they press the shutter is usually the culmination of the compositional and artistic act. There are photographers who will have nothing to do with darkroom enhancement or digital manipulation. Post-processing does offer some scope for further expressivity, but the results should always be pre-visualised and post-processing undertaken as a way to achieve that expression.

'The significant difference between photography and other art forms is its unique ability to record simply and in unbiased detail, something that is there.'
(unattributed)

Single beauty (facing opposite)

The crisp detail and strong blocks of colour that stand out from the solid black background make this single flower 'hyper real'. Strong central lighting and the forward curve of the stem and petals increase this sense of 'presence'.

Photographer: Markos Berndt.

Technical summary: Minolta Dimage 7i with macro lens, 39 sec, shot in a dark room on black background with a flashlight.

Simplify, simplify

Composition is the mental editing process a photographer applies as they work on an image to make its message easier for the viewer to read. A common mistake is to think about what to 'put into' a picture. For the beginner to photography it is tempting to lend an image import by filling it with as much detail as possible. Instead, thinking about 'what can be left out' of a picture will strengthen it. Look for the simplest theme. Simplification is an essential part of composition; getting rid of unwanted visual clutter will leave only the important elements that can then be arranged to create a well-composed image.

Photographers often pay too much attention to the subject and neglect to check for potential clutter in the background. The result is a badly organised image. A quick visual check around the edges of the subject will make certain that nothing distracting or unwanted interferes.

In-camera cropping is an often overlooked solution to the problem of simplifying an image. A zoom lens can crop the image without changing perspective as long as the photographer and subject stay put. Moving closer in fills the frame, emphasises the subject and cuts out the background. This simple technique seems surprisingly difficult for beginners to adopt.

It may not be possible to simplify the image by moving viewpoint or recomposing the image in the frame. The opportunity then presents itself to use photographic techniques such as selective focus or choosing a shallower depth of field (wider lens aperture). It may be possible to light the subject in such a way as to throw unwanted detail into deep shadow or, conversely, flood it with light.

There are numerous techniques to simplify images. Images can be simplified tonally by reducing or taking out altogether the colour in an image by using monochromatic (black-and-white) film. Alternatively, using a high- or low-key approach can be effective. This means putting the subject in a setting with light (high-key) or dark (low-key) tones. Reducing colour in an image may be possible by taking the photograph during certain atmospheric conditions (rain or mist) or by using a diffusion or fog filter on the lens. Limiting the colour palette and similar effects, such as hand-colouring, can be achieved during processing or by choosing to desaturate the colours. These techniques will be covered elsewhere later in the book (see pages 76–79 and 86–87).

'Our life is frittered away by detail…simplify, simplify.'
Henry David Thoreau (philosopher and author)

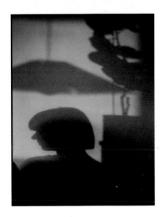

Shadow portrait (left)

An exercise in ultimate simplification, in this shot the subject has been removed altogether. Strong natural frontal lighting from a large, uncluttered window produces a well-defined shadow on the wall beside the subject, making it the focus of attention. Despite the silhouette, the image remains a portrait as it conveys the mood and character of the sitter. Enough details of the setting are retained. The small palette of rich colours comes from the late afternoon sun falling on a painted wall.

Flowers (right)

Although its colour contrasts well with the flowers, the background is cluttered with too much visible detail despite shallow depth of field from the wide lens aperture. The object in the bottom right of the frame was invisible in the camera viewfinder when it was taken. The out-of-focus vertical on the shed wall is very distracting.

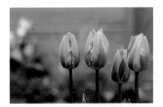

The viewpoint is closer but along the same axis, creating an unhappy shift in emphasis to the two larger out-of-focus flowers. The overlap of the flower buds in the centre and on the right isn't working.

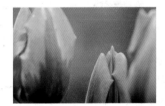

Here, the same position is retained, but the viewpoint has shifted slightly lower and to the left, which separates and simplifies the image, concentrating attention on the central flower.

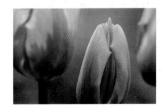

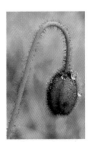
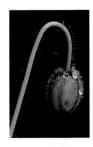

Dew (left)

This image was simplified by using a black card to remove the distracting background. The card was held far enough back to lose any incidental texture.

The golden section

Leonardo Pisano (Leonardo of Pisa) – also called Fibonacci – was a twelfth-century Italian mathematician, best known for his discovery of a remarkable sequence of numbers.

This simple numerical series starts with 0 and 1. Adding the previous two numbers in the sequence together produces the next number in the series, hence the Fibonacci numbers: 0, 1, 1, 2, 3, 5, 8, 13, 21, 34, 55, 89, 144, etc.

The ratio of each successive pair of numbers in the series (5 divided by 3, for example, is 1.666, and 8 divided by 5 is 1.6) approximates to the 'Golden Number' (1.618034), identified by the Greek letter Phi. Phi was considered the key to the secrets of heavenly mathematics. It relates to proportion, too. The Golden Number does not provide a magical solution to all problems of composition. Though people refer to the shape of an empty rectangle constructed around Golden Number proportions (1:1.618), this does not work for images cropped in these proportions where the content has a great influence. However, it does appear that we are intrinsically aware that nature is closely linked with the mathematics of sequences such as Fibonacci's and that it complies with our sense of harmony and proportion.

The Golden Section is a division based on the Golden Number proportion and can be used as a method for placing the subject in an image or of dividing a composition into pleasing proportions. It is easier to remember a ratio of 5:8 than it is 1.618, but it is much the same thing. (The name 'Golden Mean' is sometimes used to describe point of division.) Choosing where to put the horizon, fixing the main point of

interest or dividing a frame into pleasing proportions can all be done in this ratio – although of course it does not guarantee the quality of the final image.

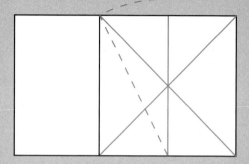

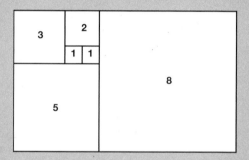

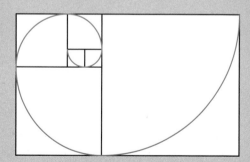

In this sequence of diagrams, the first (top) is constructed using the Golden Number proportions. The second (middle) builds a rectangle with squares based on the Fibonacci sequence. The third (above) shows a natural growth spiral that appeals to our sense of harmony.

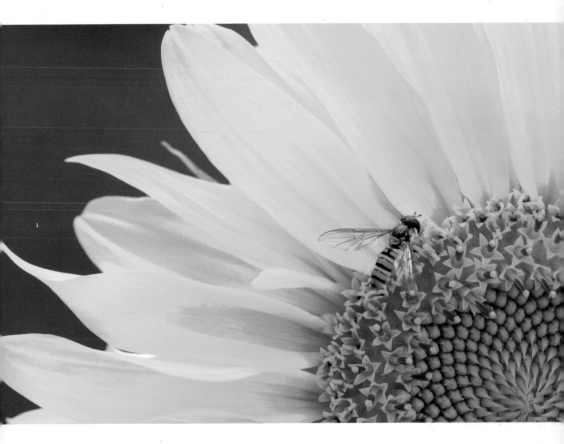

Sunflower (above)

Spirals based on the Fibonacci sequence underpin the distribution of seeds in the head of this sunflower. Plant growth, the formation of seashells – even the proportions of our bodies, reflect similar mathematical progressions.

Photographer: Nina Indset Andersen.

Technical summary: Taken on a sunny afternoon with the sun behind and to the left. A silver reflector was used to bounce light onto the subject. The blue background was originally green, but was altered in Photoshop.

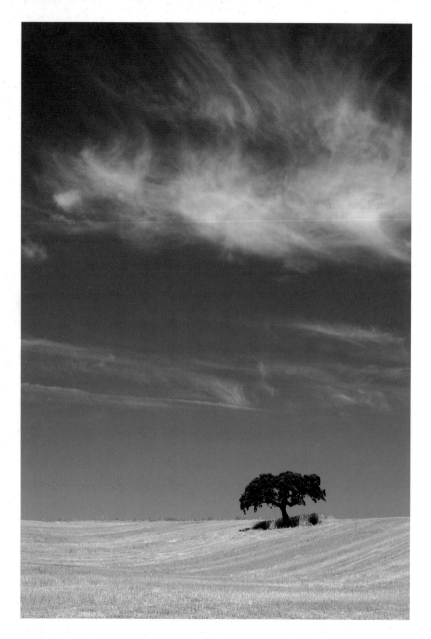

Alentejo (above)

Key elements – the tree, the optical centre of the cloud and the horizon line – are placed in accordance with geometric principles.

Photographer: Tiago Estima.

Technical summary: Canon EOS 300D, 1/125 sec at f8, ISO 100, Canon 28–105mm zoom, contrast adjusted in Photoshop.

The rule of thirds

The Rule of Thirds is little more than a simplification of the proportions of the Golden Section, but is more widely utilised by photographers. With the Rule of Thirds, the focus of interest must be placed at the intersection of lines that divide the frame into thirds from top to bottom and from left to right. The Rule of Thirds is a useful aid for establishing compositional structure in an image, but is too regular in its proportions to produce very exciting results.

Some manufacturers offer a range of grids on the display screens of their digital cameras to help the photographer with composition; some feature the conventional grid conforming to the Rule of Thirds, but others offer a grid based on a four-by-four grid, which is less useful for geometric composition. Any grid, however, provides a useful means of squaring up the camera to buildings or to the horizon line.

Dynamic symmetry

An alternative way of organising the focus of interest in a composition is to use dynamic symmetry. This is based on the proportions of the Golden Section, but determines the best place for the point of interest using diagonals rather than a grid, which some photographers find easier to visualise. Whatever the aspect ratio of the format used, draw a diagonal from one corner of the frame to the other. Then picture a line that runs at right angles to the first. With some trial and error, it becomes second nature to place subjects close to these points in the camera frame – it is important to think consciously about their precise placement if you change formats.

These geometric aids are often more useful after the fact, for cropping. Some photographers use acetate sheets with lines superimposed on them to indicate alternatives for cropping prints. These lines could also be drawn up in image-editing software as a template and used as a temporary layer to achieve a better crop.

Thirds and dynamic symmetry

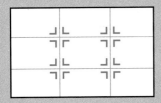

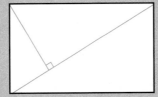

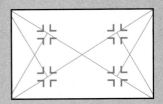

The four 'hotspots' to locate the focus of interest as dictated by the Rule of Thirds, which can be too regular to be visually exciting.

Placement of the focus of interest in an image using dynamic symmetry.

The four 'hotspots' to locate the focus of interest as dictated by dynamic symmetry.

Viewpoint

The same scene can look very different in images taken from a high versus a low viewpoint. If you imagine once again lining up your camera to take a snapshot, the camera is brought up to eye level, pointing in the general direction of the subject and an exposure is made.

So many images are taken from eye level with little consideration of the alternatives. Eye-level shots produce images with a repetitive viewpoint. In contrast, images taken on cameras with waist-level finders (twin-lens reflex models, for example) have a distinctly different feel because of the lower viewpoint.

Choosing alternative viewpoints can show mundane objects in a new or revealing way. This is one of the primary ways in which a photographer can explore a subject. A low viewpoint can include and emphasise the foreground, leading the gaze into the image from the bottom. High viewpoints can detach the viewer from the action as the gaze is forced to look downwards into the image. Extremes of high and low viewpoints can have a dislocating, but invigorating effect. Simply moving viewpoint by shifting to one side or another – rather than moving the viewpoint up or down – can create juxtapositions that might also otherwise go unnoticed.

Spiral (right)

A viewpoint directly at the centre of a stone spiral staircase emphasises perspective, depth and its repeating pattern.

Photographer: Tiago Estima.

Technical summary: Canon EOS 300D, Tamron 17–35mm SP AF f2.8–4 zoom, 1/50 sec at f4, ISO 200.

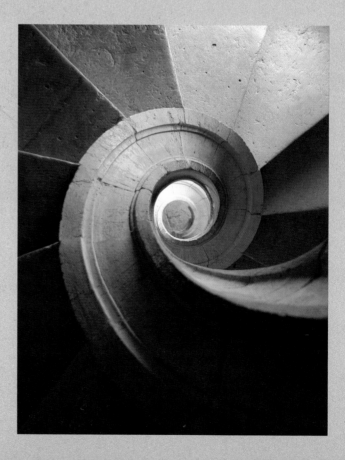

Burner (below)

Looking for a new viewpoint will take you to strange places – for example, this view of the gas burner in a hot-air balloon was taken while lying on the bottom of the basket. Strong diagonals add greater dynamism to the 'lift off' provided by the viewpoint.

Photographer: David Präkel.

Technical summary: Nikon F601 with 24–85mm Zoom-Nikkor, Kodachrome 200 Pro.

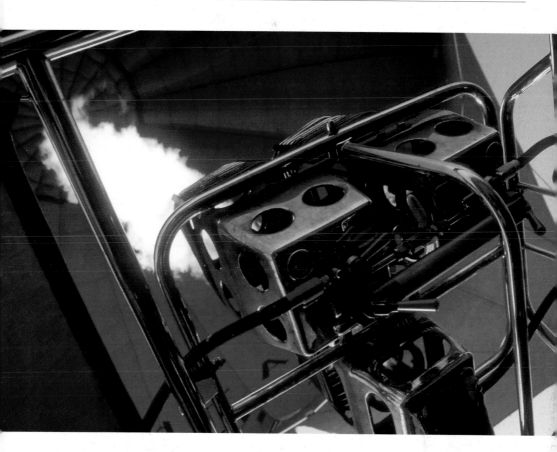

Depending on the viewpoint, the horizon can be placed high or low in the image. This will have a dramatic effect on the interpretation of the image by the viewer. A photograph of a small farm in the landscape can become either a tiny human dwelling, dominated by undulating verdant landscape or vast skies or, conversely, a prominent farmhouse dominating acres of fertile land; depending on whether the horizon is set low or high in the frame. Think carefully what you want to say about a place before you decide where to put the horizon line.

Perspective

It is not possible for two parallel kerbs at the roadside to meet in the far distance, but, to give the appearance of depth in an image that is how we draw or paint them. This is described as 'linear perspective'. The 'vanishing point' is the point in the far distance where the lines appear to meet.

Choice of viewpoint and lens focal length are major factors in the representation of depth or perspective in an image. The closer the viewpoint is to the subject, the larger it will appear in relation to more distant objects. When there are no obvious receding lines, we pick up clues to the representation of depth in a two-dimensional image in a number of ways – for example, the relative size of an object. Architects emphasise the size of a space by using repeating elements such as pillars, which seem to become progressively smaller. Other clues come from pattern or texture.

Roads and paths are represented in images as strongly angled converging lines. Looking

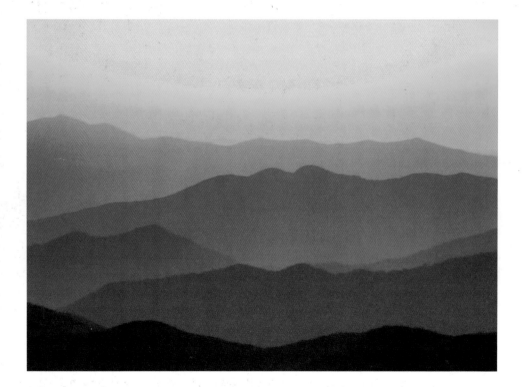

Smoky mountain sunset (above)

Aerial perspective is where distant hills are seen as lighter tones through the depths of a misty atmosphere, and overlying foreground shapes are much darker – a technique used by the Chinese artists to build depth into images. Mist and fog emphasise the effect.

Photographer: Cindy Quinn.

Technical summary: Nikon D100 with Nikon 70–200mm AFS VR lens with 3-stop hard GND filter, 1/8 sec at f22, ISO 200, spotted for sensor dust, and contrast and saturation adjusted in Photoshop.

Underground jungle (below)

Repeated and diminishing shapes and strong perspective lines produce a great sense of depth. The viewpoint puts the vanishing point dead centre, further emphasising the perspective.

Photographer: Alec Ee.

Technical summary: Nikon D70 with Nikon 18–70mm zoom, ISO 200 with slight brightness and contrast adjustment in Photoshop.

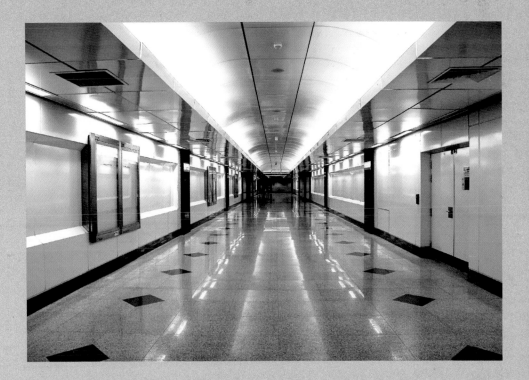

at images of rail tracks receding into the distance you may ask yourself, 'Is the train about to arrive? Or has it just left?' Any path that recedes into the image from left to right goes with the natural scanning of the eye and seems to take the gaze to its destination. A figure coming towards the viewer in such an image would seem to be 'coming back', as if walking away from something.

Buildings show the same effect where their parallel sides appear to come together; this is called 'converging verticals'. This is the inevitable result of a ground-level viewpoint. Convergence can be corrected by using a camera with a rising lens panel or a shift lens, though some small degree of convergence is needed to stop the building from looking distorted. The application of image-editing software enables a degree of correction with minimal sacrifice of quality. However, an alternative is to stress the converging verticals in the composition and exaggerate them by choosing a wide-angle lens and tipping the camera back.

Perspective and lenses

The development of formal perspective gave artists a way to represent depth in their images, to realistically portray the third dimension on the flat surface of their canvas or paper. The so-called 'standard lens' is the focal length that offers the closest perspective to 'normal' vision when viewed on a 10 x 8in print held at arm's length. 50mm is the normal 'standard' lens for 35mm cameras.

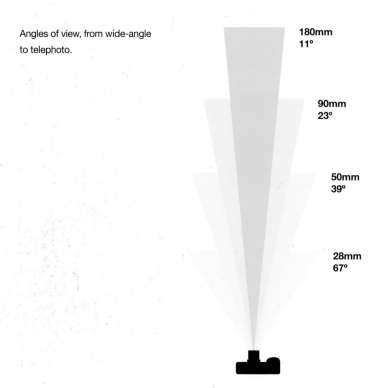

Angles of view, from wide-angle to telephoto.

180mm
11°

90mm
23°

50mm
39°

28mm
67°

Nowadays, we are used to interpreting images and accept even extreme lens perspective in images. Most people are happy to accommodate the foreshortened perspective of the long focal length lens or even the distinctive circular images produced by an ultra wide-angle fisheye lens.

A telephoto lens will flatten perspective and appear to bring foreground and background closer together. To embed an object in the environment a telephoto lens can be used to collapse perspective; very long focal-length lenses can produce apparent relationships between objects that are, in reality, quite far apart.

A wide-angle lens makes foreground objects appear much bigger than they are, and including a great deal of the background emphasises perspective effects. A zoom lens simply has variable focal length – on digital cameras this will be marked W and T for Wide and Tele.

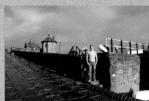
28mm

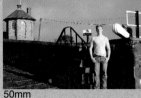
50mm

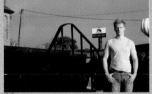
90mm

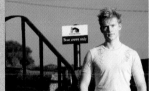
180mm

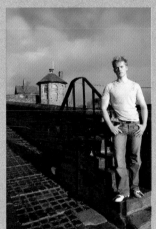
28mm

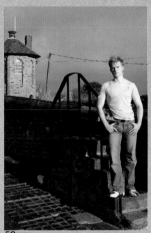
50mm

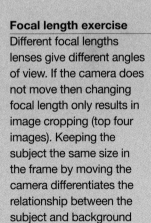
90mm

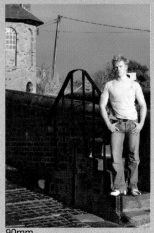
180mm

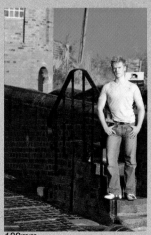

Focal length exercise

Different focal lengths lenses give different angles of view. If the camera does not move then changing focal length only results in image cropping (top four images). Keeping the subject the same size in the frame by moving the camera differentiates the relationship between the subject and background (four bottom images).

Photographer: David Präkel.

Technical summary: Nikon D100, various zoom and prime Nikon lenses. 1/250 sec at f8, ISO 200.

Perspective and the face

Lenses of different focal lengths affect images of the the human face quite radically. When taking portraits it is important to consider the effect that lens focal length has on the proportions of the face. It is no coincidence that short telephoto lenses used to be called 'portrait' lenses.

These lenses depict the face with a flattering perspective close to the way we see faces when standing at a comfortable distance – in other words, without invading their personal space. Lenses for 35mm cameras in the range 75–105mm are ideal for portraiture, and when a human head and shoulders is framed in-camera they give a good natural perspective. These semi-telephoto lenses have the additional advantage of shallower depth of field. This means that at most working apertures the background is thrown out of focus. A second reason these lenses work well for portraiture is that they allow the photographer a good working distance from the subject. An intimate portrait becomes possible without entering the personal space of the sitter, who remains relaxed and will look at ease in the final image.

Lenses with a longer focal length than 'portrait' lenses will foreshorten the perspective and give faces a flattened 'pancake' look. On the other hand, the disadvantage of wide-angle lenses is that the photographer must be physically closer to the subject to get a frame-filling portrait, which will then emphasise the part of the face closest to the camera. Viewers tend to find such images alienating. This is why compact cameras with fixed focal-length lenses are ideal for landscapes, but produce unflattering portraits. If you are working with a zoom lens, choose the telephoto end of the zoom range unless you intentionally want to produce this effect.

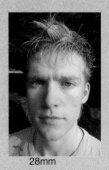 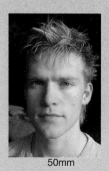 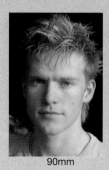 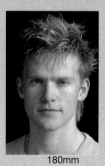

28mm   50mm   90mm   180mm

Focal length and portraiture

Lenses in the focal-length range 70–105mm (for 35mm cameras) give the face the proportions we expect from looking at another person while standing at a comfortable distance from them. Lenses of these focal lengths used to be called 'portrait' lenses. To keep the same size head and shoulders portrait with a wide-angle lens the camera must be closer to the subject, which introduces an unpleasant distortion in the proportions of the face. Similarly, a telephoto lens will flatten the perspective of the face.

Photographer: David Präkel.

Technical summary: Nikon D100 with various Nikon zoom and fixed focal length lenses, 1/60 sec at f6.7, ISO 200.

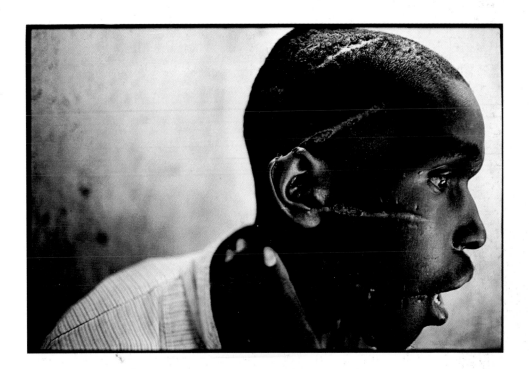

Hutu man (above)

A wide-angle lens, a close viewpoint and framing puts the viewer in uncomfortable proximity to the face of this Hutu man scarred by a machete attack. His crime was to oppose the killing of Hutu moderates and the genocide of the Tutsis in Rwanda.

Photographer: James Nachtwey/VII.

Technical summary: None provided.

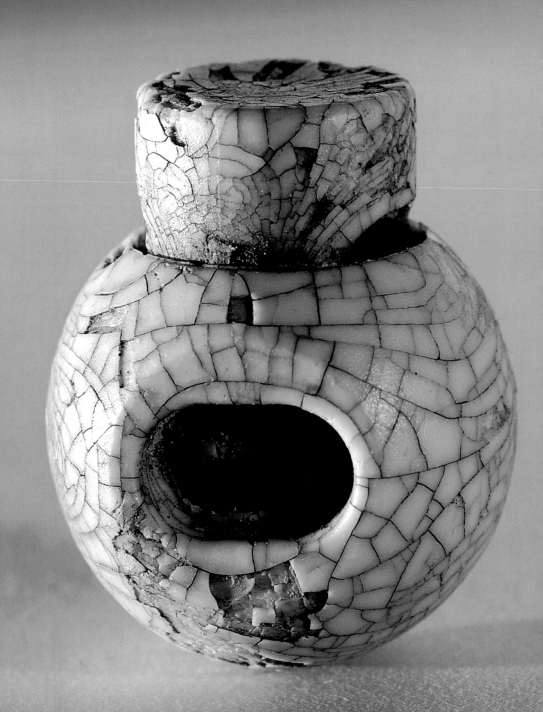

Scale

Size and scale offer lots of creative opportunities for inventive photographers. People are fascinated by extremes of size, and despite its reputation for never lying, since the earliest days of photography the camera has been used to produce images that diminish or exaggerate size.

We get our clues to size by comparison with identifiable objects in an image. Without clues to size the viewer doesn't have a reference point, and he or she must guess as to whether a thing is large or small. Landscape photographers sometimes use this technique to interesting effect by excluding the horizon from their images and framing an edited portion of the landscape, creating a world in which scale is ambiguous.

Photographers have often wilfully misled the viewer in interpreting size. Irving Penn and Patrick Tosani created images of everyday objects, such as cigarette butts and spoons. In their carefully lit close-ups these mundane items take on iconic, classic qualities, far removed from their everyday functions.

Artefact (facing opposite)

Mexican jade pot? Archaeological artefact? Choice of lighting, viewpoint and lack of reference to size and scale make this item appear much bigger and grander than it really is – a 2cm-tall, plastic anorak toggle found buried in a garden, aged by sunlight and soil!

Photographer: David Präkel.

Technical summary: Nikon D100 with 60mm Micro-Nikkor, 1/180sec at f19, two flash heads with diffusers.

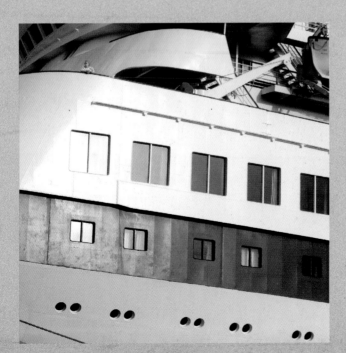

Woman and ship (left)

The massive size of this cruise liner would not be apparent if it were not for the tiny passenger seen top left – in fact, without this reference point for scale you could mistake the liner for a model. Corfu Town, Greece.

Photographer: Stephen Coll.

Technical summary: Bronica S2a Nikkor-P 200mm, Fuji Provia F 200.

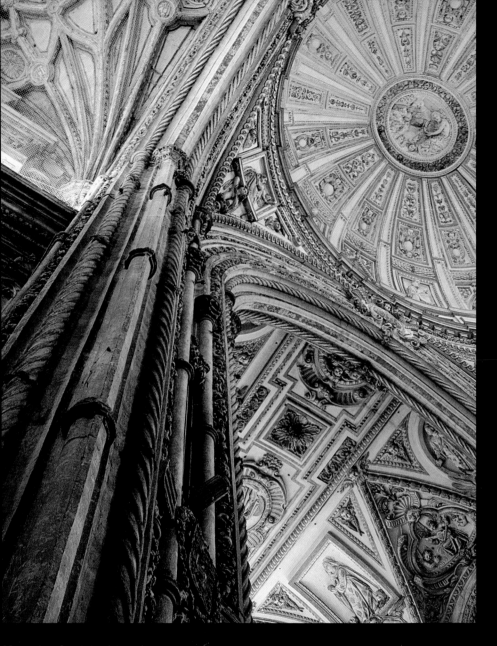

Mezquita, Cordoba (above)
All the formal elements are carefully framed, balanced and organised – columns and transept
roof of the Holy Cathedral and former mosque in Cordoba, Spain.

Photographer: Marion Luijten.

Technical summary: 24mm wide-angle lens, 1/20 sec at f6.7, ISO 800.

It is unusual to find an image that exclusively uses one of the formal elements of composition. The best images are a remarkable combination of ingredients. Looking in turn at how each of the elements can be incorporated into images will help you to understand the process of composition. In the world of fine art, the formal elements are: line, shape, form, space, texture, light and colour.

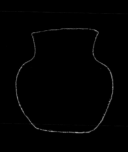

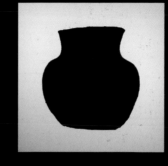

Line can either be actual marks on the paper or a boundary suggested by shapes in the image.

Shape is an area that is defined by one of the other elements, usually line, though it can also be composed of light, texture or colour. Shape has mass.

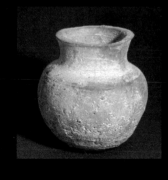

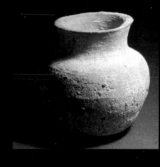

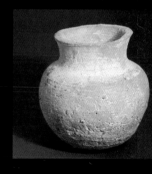

Form has volume. In two-dimensional art, adding shading to a shape gives the illusion of form. Space is two- or three-dimensional, but most often refers to the representation of the third dimension on canvas. Negative space is the absence of volume and the areas between are positive shapes.

Light is the fundamental ingredient of photography. Photographers refer to the comparative light or dark of a grey or colour as 'tone'. Artists refer to this as 'value'. In photography, changes in light levels across the surface of a three-dimensional object give the illusion of form.

Texture is a characteristic of surface revealed by the interaction of light and the surface, for example: polished metal and glass reflect brilliantly, while velvety cloth appears dull and soft. Colour can be identified as a result of human response to wavelengths of light and it affects our moods and emotions.

Point

In its purest photographic form, a point (or, in fine art terms, a mark) is the first and only place the photosensitive material changes by reacting with light – this becomes a tiny pinpoint of light on a uniform background.

Small objects can also be points. An image of a pebble on a beach is a point rather than a small area of tone. The simple point will draw attention to itself by being the only concentration of detail in an otherwise empty image. The message conveyed by the image of a single point is usually one of overwhelming isolation.

Larger areas can have a central point that functions much in the same way as a simple point. This is the virtual point at the optical 'centre of gravity' of the area of tone – much easier to visualise than to describe. The

visual centre of an evenly toned area is easy to determine, but if there is an increase in tonal or textural density, the virtual centre point will shift towards that concentration.

The placement of the point in an image can have a big impact on the way it is read by the viewer. The direction of the shadow – if one exists – can determine 'ownership of space'. The point may appear closer or seem to be static if moved near to the bottom edge of the frame.

Images are rarely composed around a single point on an otherwise uniform background. Composing with a true single point is an absurdity. By expanding the definition of point to mean a small area of concentrated detail, some of the most dramatic compositions use a point to convey information about the whole.

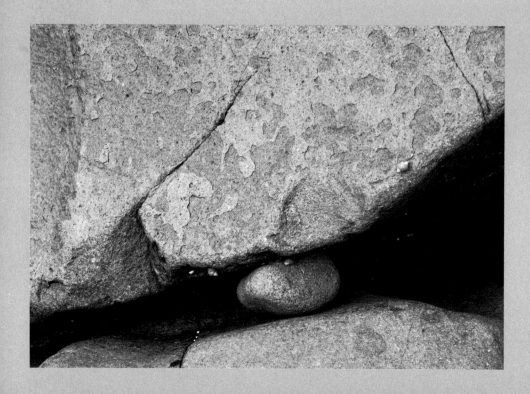

'The spot is the outcome of the first contact of the tool with the material, with the basic surface.'
Wassily Kandinsky (artist)

Tate Modern Turbine Hall, London (right)

The single point of concentrated detail is revealed as the isolated form of a man in the vast exhibition space of the Tate Modern art gallery.

Photographer: Paul Stefan.

Technical summary: Canon EOS 20D, Canon EFS 17–85 lens, 1/60 sec at f6.3, ISO 800, some local exposure control (dodging and burning) in Photoshop.

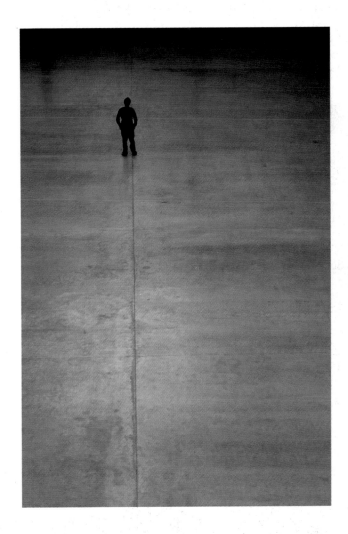

Ouch (facing opposite)

The subject is the pebble trapped in a crevice. The greater area of simply toned rock above the pebble seems to weigh down on the pebble, which introduces a new dynamic into an otherwise sparse image.

Photographer: David Präkel.

Technical summary: Nikon D100, 60mm Micro-Nikkor, 1/80 sec at f11.

Points and optical lines

Immediately a second point is introduced into an image a relationship is established between it and the existing point.

It now becomes impossible to treat the two in isolation as individual points. They are connected by a virtual line, often called an 'optical' line. In compositional terms, virtual lines are as important as actual lines.

The quality of the optical line, its direction and angle will be read as though it were a real line. This will have a bearing on the relationship between the two points. In fact, in some images, it may introduce an unintentional relationship. The optical line is the compositional equivalent of putting a set of weighing scales beneath any two objects – the gaze will move between the two, making comparisons. This tendency will intensify if the two points are in any way similar – in colour or texture for example. It may be preferable to exclude a second object from your composition precisely to avoid such a possibility. Cropping the finished image or reframing the image in-camera would then be necessary.

Depending how closely associated or widely separated the two points are within the frame, the viewer is forced to make assumptions about their relationship. This will be affected by the positioning of the virtual line between them. If two points are situated at a great distance apart in either of the top corners of the frame, the image will be read in a different way than if the same two points were positioned close together in either bottom corner.

The strongest virtual line in any image is the human gaze. We all look to see where others are looking – this is a response to both our instinct for survival and to satisfy a sense of curiosity. In portraits of two people, the relationship between the two individuals is rather like that between simple points and if there is a shared gaze the implied relationship is strengthened further.

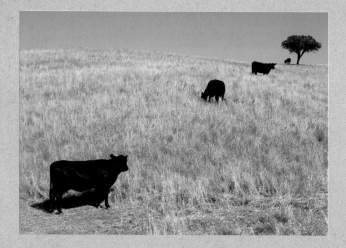

Mooh! (left)

An optical line joins the cows diagonally across the field. The tree on the horizon acts like a full stop to their 'sentence' and is given scale by the diminishing row of animals. The bulk and tone of its canopy balances the cow in the foreground.

Photographer: Jorge Coimbra.

Technical summary: Canon Powershot G3, 1/1250sec at f4.5, ISO 50.

Southern wind (below)

An optical line joins the centre of the heads of the two women. Their gaze also produces a set of optical lines to a point outside the frame. Their closeness and posture says there is something shared, but that they are for a moment distracted.

Photographer: Karl Facredyn.

Technical summary: Canon D60 with Canon 35mm 1.4L prime lens, lit only by sunlight through windows.

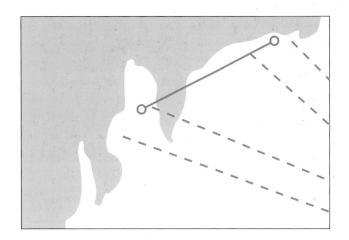

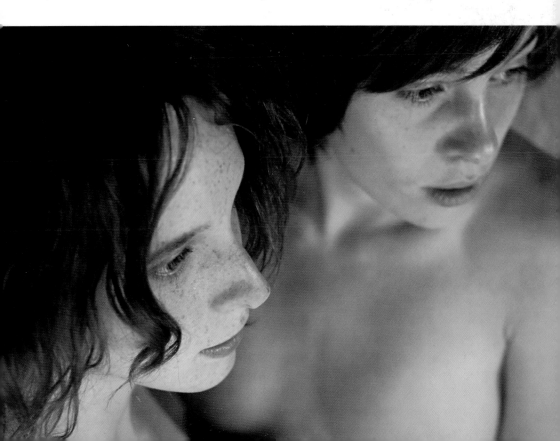

Groups

Just as two points are linked by an imaginary optical line, we create shapes from simple groups of objects – this is described by psychologists as 'closure'.

It is important when composing an image to treat the overall shape of a group and not just the individual items. Three stones in an image create a shape, a triangle. The composition will look either stable or unstable depending on the disposition of the triangle – whether the triangle itself appears stable or unstable. An inverted triangle is inherently unstable, while a wide-based triangle is strong. If you place four pebbles on a background they become joined in an invisible rectangle and the shape and its properties will provoke a response to the finished composition.

With groups of objects, the brain treats the shape created as a real-world object. If the shape formed by a group of objects appears unstable the image will seem vulnerable and transitory, which creates tension. If the arrangement of the components is stable, then the overall effect will be of strength and tranquillity. When composing images with a few distinct objects on a background – whether landscape or still life – consider the way objects are grouped and whether you want to use them to create an undercurrent of tension or a sense of calm.

One of the hardest effects to achieve in still life is to create a natural composition. Experimenting with a handful of disparate pebbles, you will discover that you start to create patterns when trying to arrange them in a 'natural' way. It is difficult to achieve a genuinely random, natural-looking arrangement. This shows how powerfully we search for pattern and structure. Selecting an odd number of items when photographing groups helps to avoid regularity.

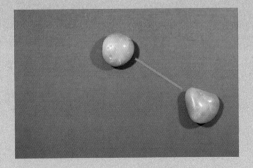

The two individual points are linked by an optical line. Given the equivalence of the two points, they can only be treated as the end points of a line.

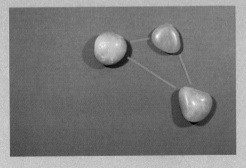

Introduce a third point and a shape emerges – in this case an unstable triangle.

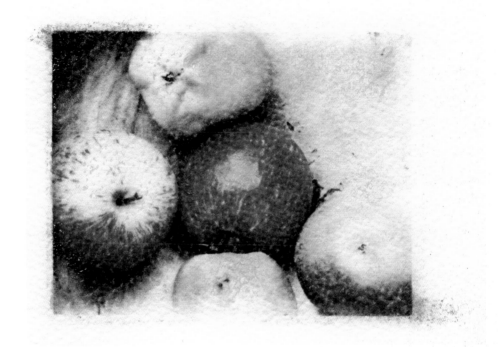

Polaroid apples (above)

A group of apples in a wooden bowl – move any one and the arrangement might collapse.

Photographer: David Präkel.

Technical summary: Polaroid Polacolor ER image transfer on Fabriano cold-pressed watercolour paper from a Kodak Elite Chrome Extra Color 100 35mm transparency.

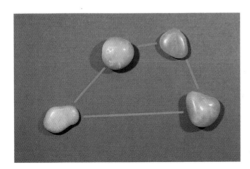

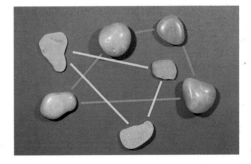

The fourth point creates a stable rectangle. Irrespective of the distance between the fourth point and the first three, the figure is not interpreted as a triangle and an isolated point. The original line has gone, although its end points have not moved.

With three more points there are two groups of points based on similar properties. The original rectangle remains, joined by an unstable triangle. A new group formation – based on similar colour or shape – will be treated as its own separate shape.

Line

Lines can be real or a virtual construct – as with the optical line that connects two points. Lines form the outlines and shapes that make up our earliest drawings on paper. It is only later, if we pursue the subject, that we learn how to sketch in tone and shadow to represent form. Even painters use simple construction lines in their underpainting and preparatory sketches. Lines can have different qualities – strong, continuous, weak and even intermittent.

Lines are really a mental construct. Our visual system, under the processing control of the brain, acts to simplify the chaotic visual jumble of the world. It does this by emphasising the edges and contours of objects while minimising areas of constant tone in a process known as 'lateral inhibition'. This begins to explain why we draw with lines, when in nature true lines are rare, and are more likely to be simply the visual boundary between one area of tone and another. The Find Edges command in Photoshop works in much the same way; finding big numerical differences in the image data that represent the edges of blocks of tone.

One of the most important lines in photography is the horizon. The sea/sky horizon is usually a true line and needs very careful alignment in images. If the horizon is an area of water and it is tilted in an unnatural way it disturbs the viewer. Water is only at rest on a truly horizontal plane. Where the true horizon lies behind a mountain range a horizon line is implied and it becomes important to level the camera with the invisible horizon to create a stable image that does not appear to be slipping off the print. It is particularly difficult to square up the camera faced with curving shorelines and mountain ranges – some photographers resort to using a bubble level on the camera body.

Some of the most dramatic lines in the everyday world are those temporarily created in the skies by the condensation trails produced by jet aircraft. For photographers trying to compose a timeless landscape image these lines are a nuisance, but they can add drama to a skyscape. Overhead power and phone lines can also be successfully built into an image.

There are often few true lines in our images (1 and 3) as many lines are really boundaries between areas of tone (2 and 4).

1

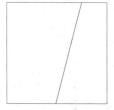

2

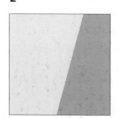

3

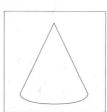

4

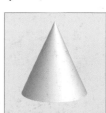

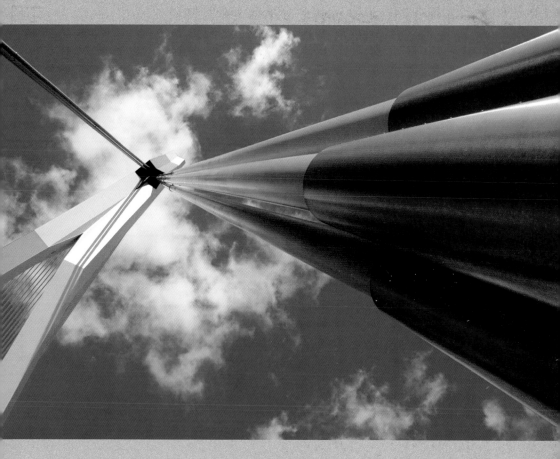

Skyward (above)

This unexpected viewpoint looks directly up at the lines of the graceful cable-stay Swan Bridge (Erasmusburg) that joins north and south Rotterdam. Lines radiate from a carefully placed single point of interest into the four corners of the frame.

Photographer: Wilson Tsoi.

Technical summary: Nikon D70 with Nikkor 18–70mm, f3.5–4.5G, AF-S, 1/160sec at f16, ISO 200, with a little warmth added using Colour Balance in Photoshop.

The meaning of lines

Just as we treat images of objects as stand-ins for the real thing, we treat lines in an image as though familiar, real-world forces such as gravity or the wind act upon them.

There are two states of balance for straight lines; vertical lines are one. They represent a balance of forces and are static. Forces are in balance to keep the line upright.

A gently curved line shows the action of unequal forces bending the line over to one side – the greater the curvature, the greater the apparent force. We know the direction of the force from what we know of nature – that the line bends away from the force. The curved line is stable, but giving way to the force acting upon it.

Angled lines are dynamic. They are most unstable around 45 degrees – the line appears about to fall flat at any moment.

Sinuous, S-shaped lines are known as beauty or 'Serpentine' curves. Their interpretation can depend on their orientation in the frame; arranged vertically they reflect strength and dynamic balance, like muscles acting on each other. Across the frame, they are undulating like hills or rivers through a landscape or the soft curves of a reclining body. They show the action of great forces moving slowly.

Zigzag lines are evidence of a disruptive force, and are interpreted variously as exciting, angry or unsettling. They represent concentrated energy.

Horizontal lines are the most stable. They respond to gravity and are at rest and motionless.

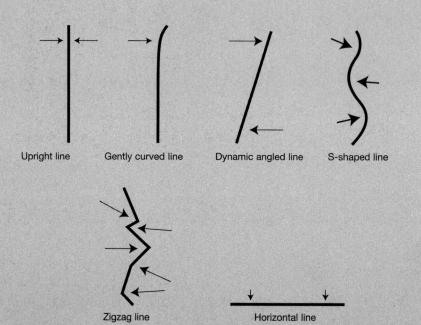

Upright line   Gently curved line   Dynamic angled line   S-shaped line

Zigzag line   Horizontal line

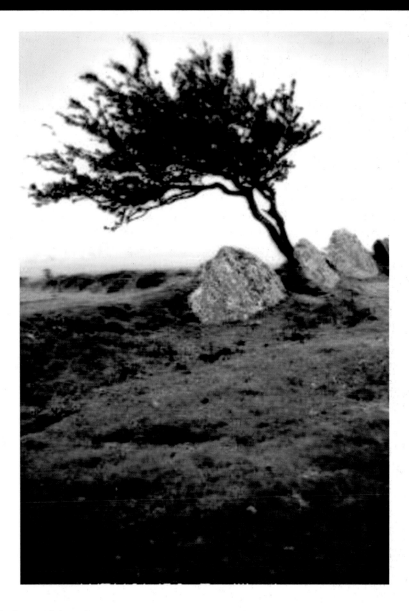

Invisible forces (above)

The dynamic tension of this image relies on the shape and angle of the tree created by the reaction to the strong forces of wind and weather. Compositional interest is added by the fact the tree seems to have taken on the shape of the rock below it as if it has been moulded by some unseen force.

Photographer: Michael Trevillion, Trevillion Images.

Technical summary: Olympus OM1 with 50mm lens, 1/125 sec at f8, Kodak 35mm infra red film, slight burning-in of sky, a bit of soft focus filtering during print exposure in the darkroom.

Diagonals

Angled lines impart some degree of
movement. Diagonals are a special case.
They are lines that run roughly from one
corner of an image to another. They give the
feeling that the line is displaced. This creates
a feeling of expectation, movement and
tension in what would otherwise be a static
image. They need not be actual lines, as
points in diagonal arrangements appear to
move down the optical line that joins them.

Diagonals appear in images in one of two
ways. Diagonal lines in the real world can
be photographed in their true orientation.
Alternatively, lines that are horizontal or
vertical in the real world can be canted over
to the diagonal. Tipping an image over in the
frame has become photographic shorthand
for energy and dynamism, sometimes
disorientation. Just cropping an image of a
stationary vehicle on the slant will make it
appear to be moving.

In Western culture, our eyes are accustomed
to scanning a page of text from top left to
bottom right. We treat empty rectangles in
much the same way. Diagonal lines that run
with the gaze reflect a sense of order, but do
not have the same impact as those that run
counter to our gaze. Diagonals that run from
bottom left of the image to top right are
considered more dynamic and give greater
sense of movement.

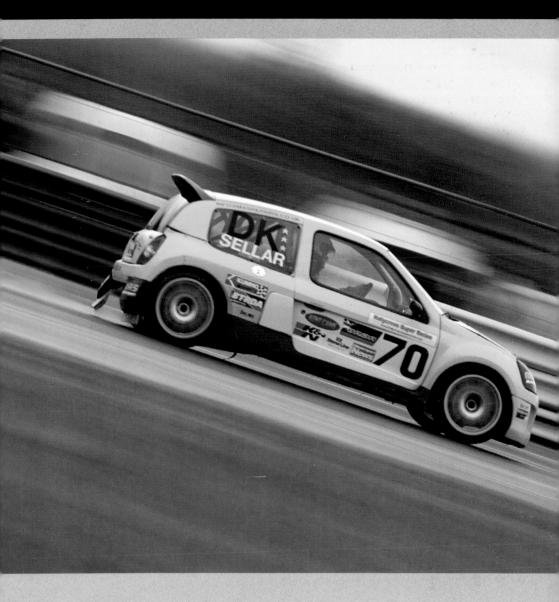

Grand Prix, British Rallycross (above)

Although it is usual to leave some space in front of a moving object, Elsworth places the subject at the bottom of the slope and as close to the frame edge as possible to accentuate speed. Careful pre-focus and panning with the autofocus off captures the subject sharp even at slow shutter speed.

Photographer: David Elsworth.

Technical summary: Nikon D100 with Sigma 70–300mm lens, ISO 400, 1/20sec at f8.

Curves

A simple curve can have dynamism, but somehow it calms and slows down the action. Because of their close association with the curves of the human body and with gently rolling hills and valleys, we connect curved lines with beauty and the sensual.

The 'line of beauty', about which the artist William Hogarth wrote at length, is a double curve or flat S shape (a 'compound' as opposed to 'simple' curve). The ideal is said to be the curve where the lower back joins the upper buttocks – which is much the same in a man or woman. Aligned vertically, this compound curve looks perfectly balanced. Gravity runs through it but the curve seems to resist the force. The beauty curve is also referred to as a 'cyma' curve (from the Greek, meaning 'wave'). Sensuous curves are produced where water wears

down rock with the action of the waves. Photographers have found water-worn rock a rich source of images that are sympathetic with the human form. There is a satisfying harmony and stillness in these curves.

When the S shape lies in the perspective plane of the image and is foreshortened – in, for example, an image of a meandering river, it suggests natural, unhurried progression. It lends a feeling of timelessness without the image appearing to be static. A real or absolute line is not needed, only the suggestion of the curve by careful placement of points of interest.

Two beauty curves together can suggest pulchritude, kissing lips or, if reflected back to back, the upward flickering of the flame.

Eleanor 1947 (facing opposite)

One of Callahan's series of nude images of his wife, in which the female form is brilliantly reduced to the simplicity of a gently curved upright line with smaller lines branching off. The crop around the subject abstracts it slightly, forcing the viewer to question what it might be.

Photographer: Harry Callahan.

Technical summary: None provided.

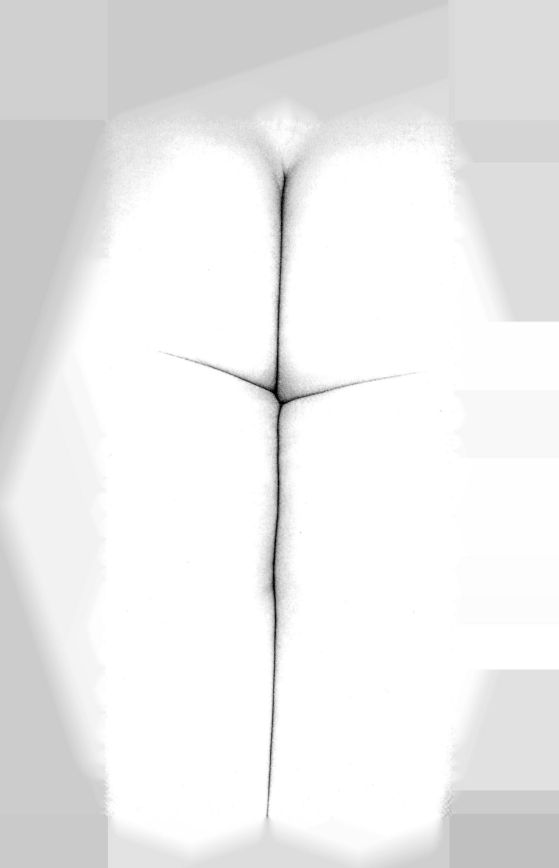

Leading lines

The concept of the 'leading line' is one of the earliest in photographic composition. It is also one of the hardest to discredit, despite being challenged by scientific evidence.

Leading lines, which are meant to entice the eye to the real subject, are a photographic myth. As long ago as 1973, Andreas Feininger, one of the best photographic writers of his day, wrote: 'The entire theory of leading lines is a fallacy.' Yet, the idea is still presented as 'fact' in photographic magazine articles and on websites today. Research studies, using miniature cameras to record eye-movements, show that we do not look for lines, real or otherwise, in images. In fact, our gaze is more attracted to angles than to straight lines. Viewers often 'enter' the picture at small areas of high contrast (potentially significant features) looking straight at the part of the picture that first 'catches their eye'.

When we look at a picture the order in which we scan the different elements varies considerably – as does the time we spend scanning for and looking at each element. Experiments on human eye movement show that viewers spend most of their time looking at parts of an image that have the most detail, contrast or curvature. The viewer may see other things in your images than your subject. He or she may be interested in entirely different aspects of the subject than what you intended to show.

Presented with accompanying captions, the viewer can be predisposed to scan images in a particular way. (What a viewer also brings in terms of culture has a major impact on what they 'see' in a picture.) The viewer treats portraits in much the same way as another human face, focusing on eye contact, except that with an image the gaze is not returned, so the relationship is much less intense. The painting, opposite, by Ilya Repin, a Russian Naturalist painter, was subjected to an experiment by Russian physiologist Alfred Yarbus to determine the patterns of just this kind of 'seeing'.

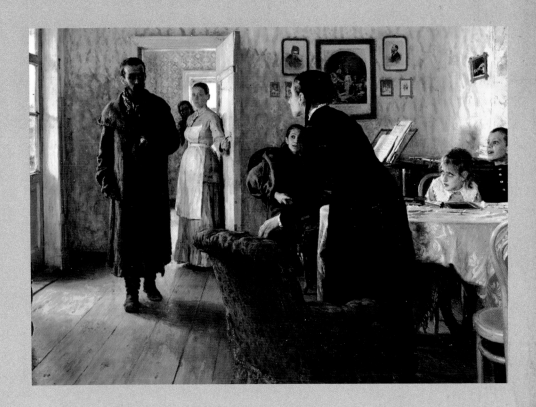

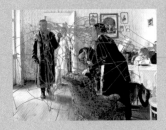

1

Without any instructions, the viewer's eyes scanned the picture. It was concluded that viewers did not use the strong perspective lines of the floorboards as 'leading lines'.

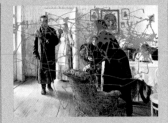

2

This scan pattern shows how a viewer looked at the picture when asked to judge the wealth and standing of the family depicted in the painting.

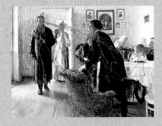

3

This shows the eye-movement pattern produced when the viewer was asked to estimate the ages of the characters in the painting.

Shape

Shape is usually defined by one of the other formal elements, such as line. Shapes are even described as being delineated, but shape can also be composed of an area of even or gradually changing tone.

A pool of light, a patch of texture or splash of colour all present as shape. What has already been said about curves and zigzag lines applies equally to curved and jagged shapes.

As with literal and optical lines there can be literal and virtual shapes in our images. In the section on Groups, page 42, we saw how shapes are created by points formed at the corners of shapes, enclosing an otherwise plain area of background. And, just as we look for faces in a fire, our active visual-processing system loves the challenge of ambiguity and tries to work out the puzzle by looking for recognisable shapes.

Artists treat shapes as either being geometric or natural shapes. Abstract shapes are generally natural forms that have been simplified in some way. Many photographers have studied natural organic shapes to find the underlying geometry.

A common device is to photograph an object that has the shape of another – a cloud that looks like a face, for example. These images have the same attraction as optical illusions based on the reversal of a human face or figure and something else entirely – the fascination stems from not being able to see both forms of the image at once.

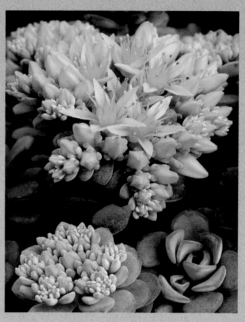

Succulent triangle (above)
Three optical centres produce a stable triangular arrangement, while the inverted triangle of colour above introduces an unstable dynamic into this close-up photograph of three stages of flower growth in a succulent.

Photographer: David Präkel.

Technical summary: Nikon D100, 60mm Micro-Nikkor, low, summer evening light, 1/10 sec at f32.

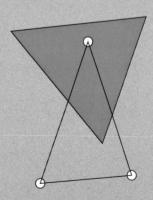

A stable and unstable triangle arrangement.

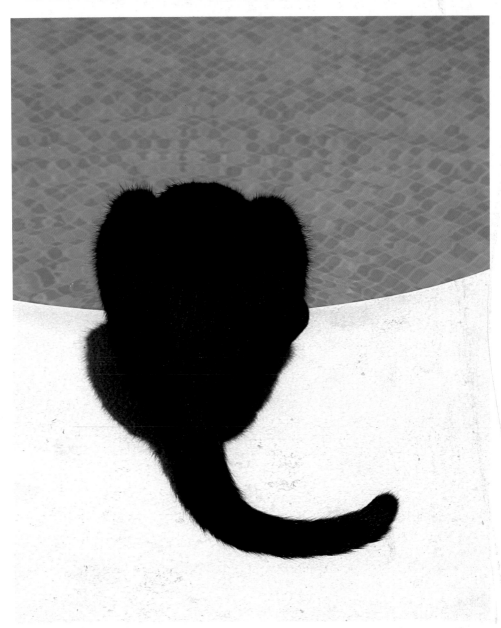

Pose (above)

The picture has 'incident'. Once we make out the simplified shape of the black cat, we know that a cat in this posture is just poised to spring.

Photographer: Jorge Coimbra.

Technical summary: Canon Powershot G3, 1/800 sec at f8, ISO 50.

Dominance of size and tone

In any image, two areas of roughly the same size and tone will appear to be in balance. The balance will tip in favour of either a larger area, an area with greater density of information (more detail) or one that is markedly darker or lighter than the rest of the picture.

Painters refer to this quality as 'attraction'. Some elements will attract more attention than others. Shape, lines, tone, form, pattern density and complexity, colour – all play a part in the balancing act, which is difficult to quantify, but easier to identify in well-composed images.

Position also plays an important role. Given the same two elements, the one nearest the edge will be treated as having greater 'attraction'. Every part of the image has some degree of attraction and even an 'empty' background will have some aspect of tonal gradation or even 'suggestion' of what is not or what could be there. Individual points – especially similarly sized or toned points – will be associated by the viewer and will be assessed, from the point of view of balance, as a single entity.

The eye naturally seeks balance in an image and this can be either static or dynamic. Static balance is found in purely symmetrical images with their equal elements placed on either side of a central line or pivot – these images, their strengths and weaknesses, are covered later in the book. Dynamic balance is achieved when items with unequal attraction are given some equivalence. This can be done by increasing the attraction of one by putting it near an important locus within the frame (the point of interest 'hotspots') or near to the frame's edge.

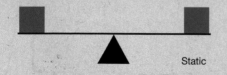

Static

When formal elements are present in equal quality/quantity around a central line – the 'pivot point' or 'fulcrum' – the picture is described as being in 'static balance'. It may be pleasing to look at, but there will be no drama.

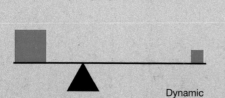

Dynamic

An image can still be in balance when formal elements are present in unequal quantities/qualities if the balance point of the picture is shifted. Here, a small, dense object balances a larger, lighter object. This is known as 'dynamic balance' and it lends drama and tension to an image.

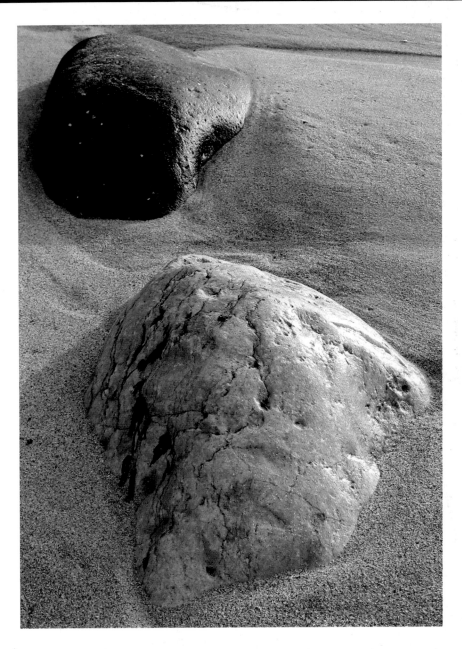

Balance (above)

Dynamic balance applied to the foreground and background of an image. Balance is not to be judged across a horizontal line in an image, but in the planes of the image itself. A darker, small object in the distance will balance a lighter, larger object in the foreground.

Photographer: Jorge Coimbra.

Technical summary: Canon Powershot G3, 1/250 sec at f4, ISO 50.

Negative shapes

If people are presented with a completely homogeneous field of view they become disoriented – pilots and skiers sometimes report this in 'white out' weather conditions. Our visual system needs something on which to fix.

Our visual world consists of numerous instances of subjects seen against their backgrounds. We choose the subject depending on our motivation. What a photographer would refer to as 'subject' and 'background' is what a psychologist would call 'figure' and 'ground'. Artists would refer to the same idea as 'positive' and 'negative' shape. If the subject of the photograph is the positive shape, then the background is the negative shape. The optical illusion of figure and ground immediately produces tension. This is because the brain, unable to hold on to both negative and positive shapes, can't decide which is the most important.

Choice of viewpoint can distinguish between or emphasise the relationship between subject and background. When taking a picture, positive and negative shapes can be enhanced by lighting to produce wide tonal separation between the subject and background. High-contrast film or custom contrast curves on a digital camera can be used to enhance the difference. At printing stage, high-contrast photographic paper can reduce the shading and fine textures that contribute to the appearance of form. The manipulation of contrast and threshold gives much the same control with digital images.

Ambiguous (left)

Figure/ground reversal in a real photograph – it is a hand, but are the fingers light or dark?

Photographer: David Präkel.

Technical summary: Nikon D100 Nikon, 70–300mm zoom, 1/125 sec at f4, ISO 200, deliberately defocused.

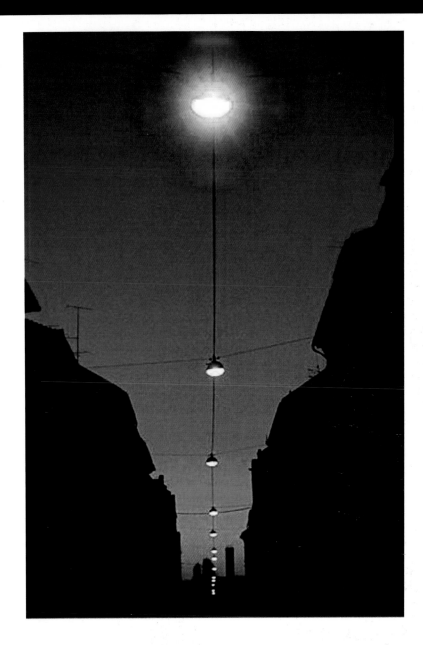

Streetlights (above)

Though the centrally placed row of streetlights is the formal subject of this image, the negative shape of the late evening sky, as defined by the silhouette of the buildings, plays a large part in its attractiveness.

Photographer: Mellik Tamas.

Technical summary: Fuji Finepix S2 Pro, 60mm Micro-Nikkor lens, 1/45 sec at f4.8, ISO 400, some cropping, sharpening and increase in saturation in Photoshop.

Form

A shape defined by lines, colour changes or areas of pattern and texture is still a two-dimensional object in an image. It covers an area and is described as having 'mass'. What makes a shape take on form is the introduction of shading within its boundaries. Form is the representation of the third dimension in the two dimensions of the flat image.

Tonal gradation

We understand how light falls on three-dimensional objects from observation. We process the information from highlights and shadows to create a mental map of an object, which enables us to grasp it in our hand rather than putting our hand through the shape. The richer the information the photographer captures about the way the light falls on an object, the more realistic the representation of the object will be to the viewer. The viewer also takes some cue as to the emotional mood of a picture by the positioning of the main light. The higher the highlight on an object, the higher the 'sun' is in the sky. Conversely, low-angle lighting will be interpreted as 'evening' and evoke tranquillity.

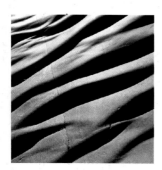 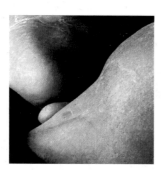 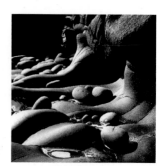

Beach forms (above and facing opposite)

Astute photographic observations of form. Shadows and highlight play an important role in creating the appearance of a sensuous three-dimensional world, enhanced by the colours and texture. Such close observation triggers a response to treat these geological formations as if they were flesh and blood.

Photographer: Stephen Coll.

Technical summary: 1954 Rolleicord 75mm Xenar Ektachrome 400 and 1960 Bronica S2a with Nikkor 75mm, Fuji Provia F 400.

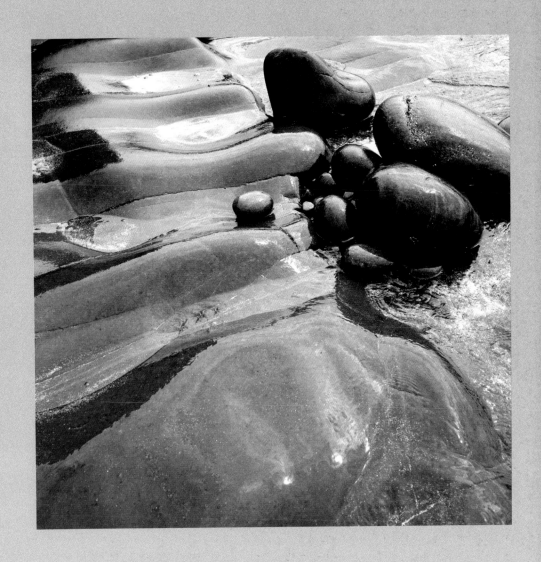

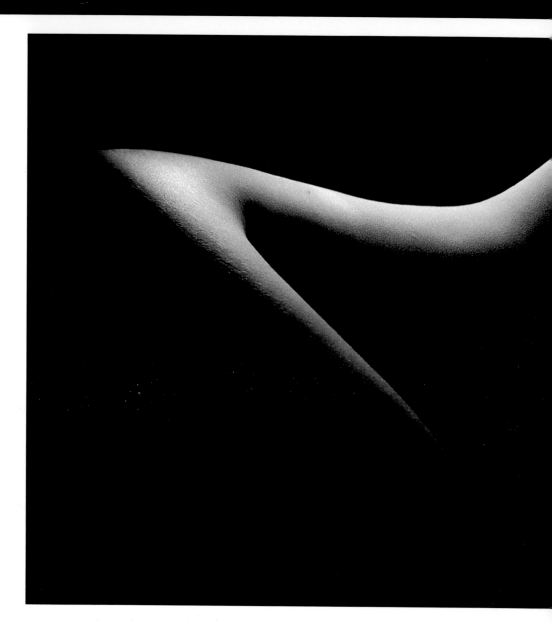

Bodyland (above)

The simplest photographic vocabulary – the subtlest grading of tonal values – can say so much, creating a strong emotional reaction in the viewer.

Photographer: Tomas Rucker.

Technical summary: Fuji Finepix S5000 compact, 1/140 sec at f2.8, ISO 200.

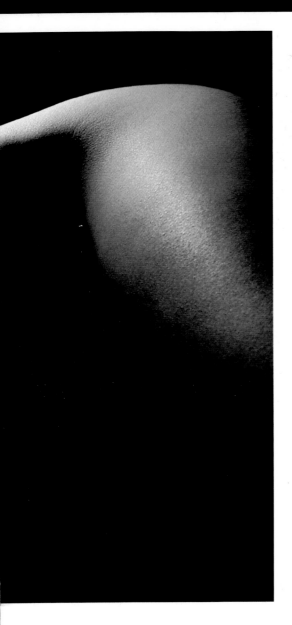

Shape plus tone

The quality of form is down to the subtlety with which the photographic medium portrays tone. Information about tone is in the density of silver grains in film or in a digital number code. Fine-grain film is a guarantor for subtle tonal information and the bigger the negative area, the better. This explains why the 5 x 4in negative and view camera are still favourites with many flower or figure photographers where capturing subtlety of tone is key.

With the digital medium it is not quite as simple as more pixels means smoother tonality. The quality of digital image processing in-camera has as much to do with the quality of tonal information as raw pixel count – older 4–5MPx professional and semi-professional cameras produce a smoother tonality than more recent 7–8MPx consumer models. The physical size of the pixels on the digital sensor and its inherent noise also play a part in how clean the image appears.

Digital post-processing can lose tonal information, especially if information has to be made up (interpolated) by the computer when levels or curves are coarsely adjusted – the existing tonal information is stretched to cover a wider range of tones, and banding (posterisation) can occur that reduces the smoothness and subtlety of the tonal range. The average human eye can see more than 65, but probably less than 100 different shades of grey. Digital systems would seem safe with 256 levels of grey, or 8-bit, but you can push the boundaries by choosing 16-bit grey, which offers a greater safety margin and better mathematical precision for manipulations.

Overcoming the limitations of 2D
Many of the art movements of the twentieth century struggled with what were considered by many to be the limitations of realist art. The Cubists challenged the notion that art should reflect nature.

They turned their collective back on the traditional depiction of perspective and instead attempted to simplify form into simple geometric solids (the 'cube' of Cubism) using multiple viewpoints in their images. Artists such as Picasso and Braque influenced Alfred Stieglitz and his circle of photographers in America. Vorticist paintings looked like superimposed photographs manipulated to form swirling, moving forms in the static world of the canvas.

In the early 1970s, the Yorkshire-born artist David Hockney experimented with Polaroid instant cameras to produce explorations of reverse perspective and made reference to Picasso's Cubist paintings. Hockney tried to break through the two-dimensional bounds of the photograph by capturing a series of images taken around an object. He experimented with 'reverse' perspective, creating striking portraits which looked as though the skin had been unwrapped from the subject.

Early on, Hockney created montages of component images in a structured grid and later in a more organic style. He called these images 'joiners'. Intriguingly, as he shot the images, he was also recording the passing of time. His joiners are a combination of images of the same subject taken from different viewpoints at different times.

Digital cameras are uniquely convenient for shooting sequences of images that explore the three-dimensional nature of an object. Imaging software makes it easy to create a blank digital canvas and to drop in the various images to create a 'joiner'.

Ian washing his hair, London, January, 1983 (facing opposite)
This 'joiner' expands both space and time to create a complex narrative within the image.
Photographer: David Hockney.
Technical summary: None provided.

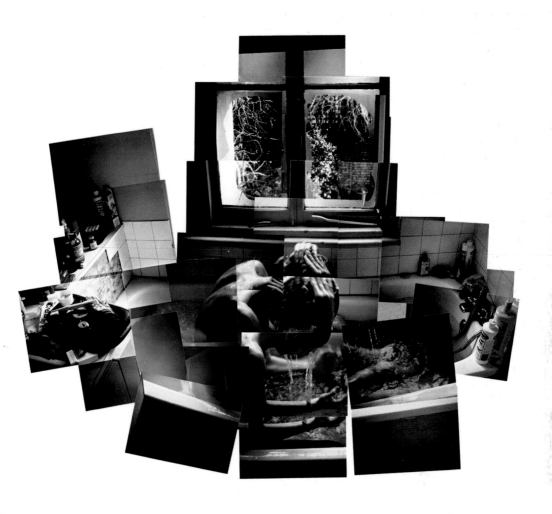

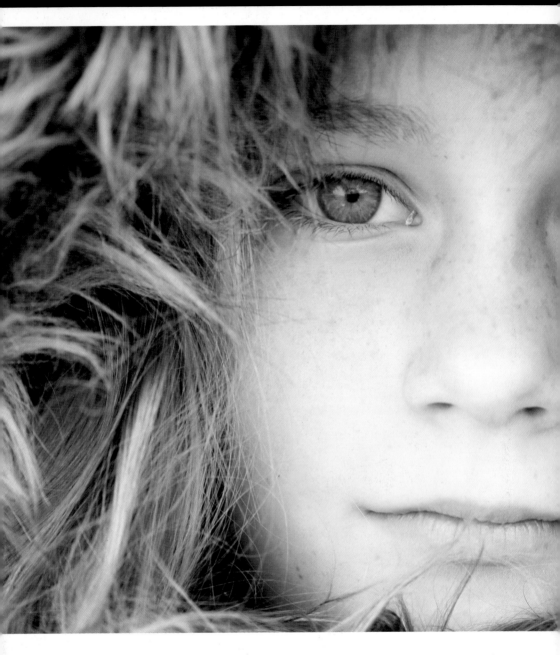

Emilie (above)

Texture need not mean rough wood and rock. Diffuse frontal light and a shallow depth of field (critically focused on the eyes) flatter the smooth skin textures of this young sitter and the soft fur of the hood.

Photographer: Nina Indset Andersen.

Technical summary: White balance was adjusted in converting the RAW digital file to give a colder light.

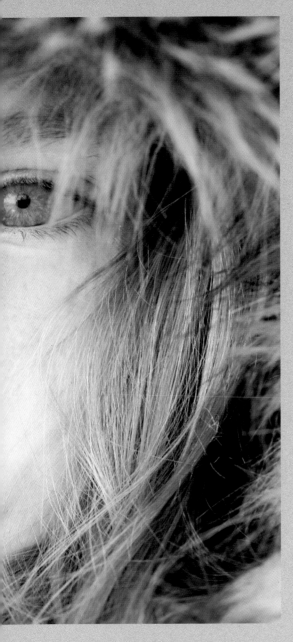

Texture

Sight and touch are very closely related senses. Because of this strong connection, developed in our infancy, the visual representation of texture can generate a strong emotional response through association or memory. In many viewers, the high-contrast texture of reptile skin will evoke quite a different reaction from softly lit wool. The photographer can exaggerate texture to evoke emotion or can choose lighting conditions that reduce the appearance of texture when it is not wanted.

When we talk about texture, we often mean the surface area of objects such as rock or wood, but texture in an image can mean much larger or more expansive features of landscape, for example the furrows of a ploughed field seen from a distance. The differences between textures helps the viewer to appreciate depth and perspective in an image. Just as the archaeological photographer waits for slanting light to reveal the shadow of a long-buried village, the landscape photographer waits for the sun to illuminate the textures of sand dunes, rocks, and cultivated fields.

In portraiture, care must be taken with the angle of light so as not to unduly emphasise skin texture if it is not appropriate to the image. High-contrast, side lighting can add years to the appearance of skin. Softening the light and angling it directly onto the subject reduces the effect.

Angle and quality of light

When light falls across the surface of an object at an angle it reveals its texture – the shallower the angle, the more prominent the texture. Direct lighting illuminates the tiny peaks and troughs of a textured surface evenly, which reduces the appearance of texture. Side or 'raking' light casts deep shadows that enhance the texture of an object. If the texture has a 'grain' – wood or skin, for example – the lighting should always be angled at right angles to the run of the grain to fully reveal the texture.

The quality of light also plays a part. The important aspect is not the colour or direction of the light but whether it is diffuse or focused, 'omni-directional' (spreading in all directions) or from a single source. Some light sources cast hard shadows, while others create softer shadows – each reveals the texture of a surface differently. Soft boxes and available light through a window, for example, produce 'flattering' light. This 'soft' lighting is frequently used in portrait, glamour and fashion photography where the skin texture is important. Conversely, a spot light throws hard light on a subject, producing hard-edged shadows which are useful for adding character to a face.

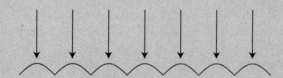

Light hits the surface at right angles illuminating peaks and valleys evenly.

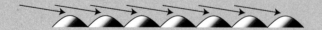

Light hits the surface at a shallow angle so that each peak casts a shadow in the next valley – micro contrast (texture).

Driftwood (facing opposite)

Low evening light picks out the wood grain and worn paint in this fence made from driftwood in Kippford, Scotland.

Photographer: David Präkel.

Technical summary: Nikon D100 with 60mm Micro-Nikkor, 1/90 sec at f4.8.

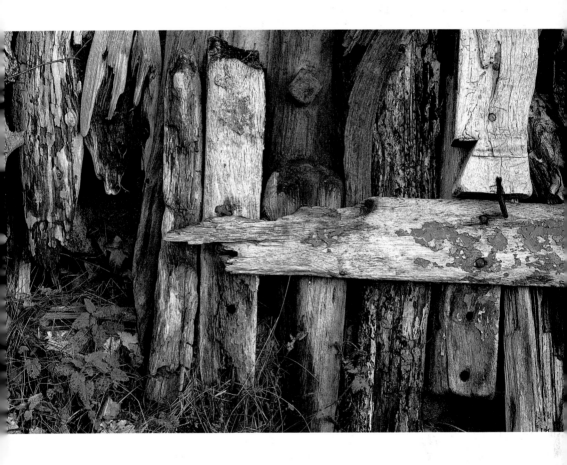

Grain and noise

Beyond the texture of the subject and of lighting, the medium can contain its own texture. Black-and-white film is composed of clusters of silver halide crystals and colour film is composed of tiny clouds of dye.

Film that is more sensitive to light is composed of coarser grains. Grain lends structure and many black-and-white photographers consider that grain adds value to an image. Aficionados talk about 'gritty' photographs, which are high-contrast, grainy images often associated with social documentary photography.

Digital has its 'grain', too – this is called noise. When a digital camera takes long exposures in low light, the background noise of the sensor itself is nearly as big as the signal (the picture) that is being recorded. The sensors in digital cameras are analogue devices, which sample the image, divide it up into pixels and measure the power of the red, green and blue components of each of these picture elements – this information only becomes digital after it leaves the sensor in an analogue-to-digital converter. The sensor's inherent background noise can break up the image with pixel values that are 'out of place' – hence, visual 'noise'. Digital photographers more often consider noise to be detrimental to the quality of an image. They employ noise-reduction software to reduce the effects.

However, noise can enhance an image. Digital noise can even be added to an image at a later stage using image-editing software. Many professional digital cameras have high-sensitivity settings that can be used to produce lots of 'chroma', or colour, creating an effect similar to the coloured grain of high-speed colour film.

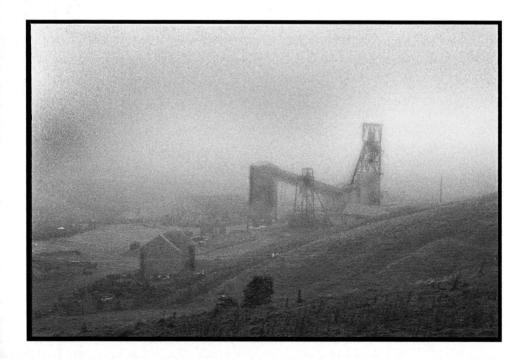

Pictish man (right)

This small fragment of a Pictish carving of a saint lay in the dark corner of a museum cabinet. High digital chroma (colour) noise was a bonus for this subject.

Photographer: David Präkel.

Technical summary: Nikon D100 with 60mm Micro-Nikkor, ISO 6400, 1/60sec at f4.

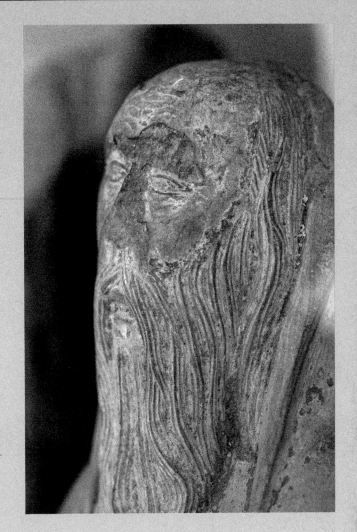

Grove Rake mine (facing opposite)

The film grain adds to the exceptionally heavy rain in this image of the remains of the last working fluorite mine in the high North Pennines, UK.

Photographer: David Präkel

Technical summary: Leica R8 35–70mm with Vario-Elmar zoom, Kodak TMax 3200, digital brown tone.

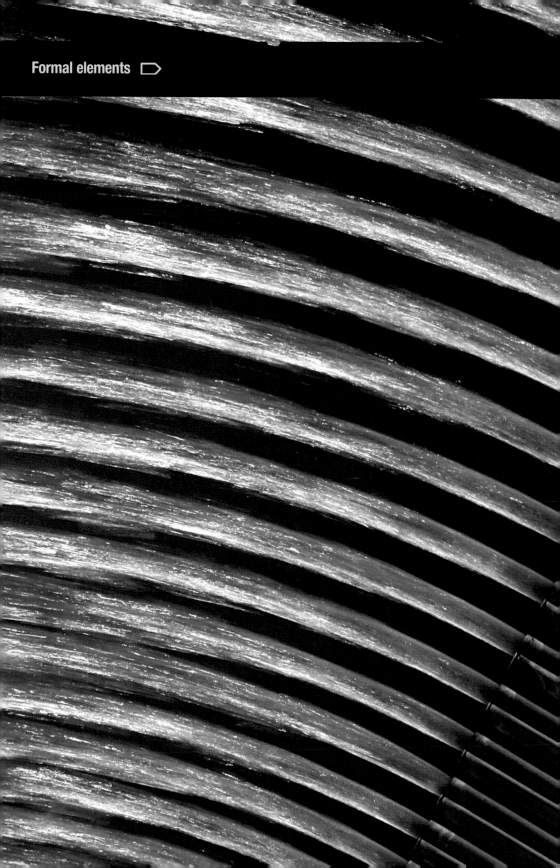

Pattern

Humans are fascinated by pattern. When we look at anything, the receptor cells in the retina react specifically to certain lines, angles, colour and movement under the organising control of the visual cortex in our brains. The appeal of visual puzzles and eye-catching quality of interlocking patterns demonstrates this. Our brains are programmed to compare the elements of pattern and to look for differences.

Pictures containing patterns must feature something more than simple repetition. It can be easily over-done and becomes a compositional cliché. The challenge for the photographer is to capture the rhythms and variations of alternating pattern in an image, while also saying something about the subject being photographed. Perversely, what attracts the viewer's attention is when expectations are not confirmed – when the pattern breaks, for example.

Pattern can even be used to reveal form. Light coming through repeating structures, such as fences or windowpanes, creates fascinating shapes as each repeated block of the pattern falls onto and wraps around the solid form. A very fine repeating pattern will look like a texture.

The urban landscape is full of geometric, repeating patterns, while nature offers a more random arrangement of quite complex patterns that can be harder to interpret.

Water abstract (facing opposite)

A pattern made by the arcing water spouts of a fountain is made more interesting by the unique details of each jet. The choice of viewpoint and lens focal length lends immediacy. The image highlights the striking contrast between the curves of the water and the straight lines of the metal pipes, a detail that can go unobserved.

Photographer: Tiago Estima.

Technical summary: Canon EOS 300D with Canon 28–105mm f3.5–4.5 zoom, 1/30 sec at f22, ISO 100.

Tone

Increased contrast in an image simplifies shape and emphasises strong textures. Lower levels of contrast soften tone, reduce the appearance of texture and can change the mood of an image. Contrast can also be manipulated to creative effect at printing stage.

Tone refers to the full gamut of greys – all the shades from solid black to paper white. A subject with a full range of tones has normal contrast. In black-and-white photography, the degree of contrast in the printing paper is selected to match the contrast in the negative to produce a print with a full scale of tones. Variable contrast papers, which alter contrast under different combinations of yellow and magenta light, make this easy in the darkroom. A low-contrast print is composed largely of light greys and dark greys. The degree to which a low-contrast image is successful depends very much on the subject of the image. Low-contrast images evoke tranquillity. High-contrast images contain more extremes between black and white with very little mid-tone information. They are attention-grabbers and their graphic nature can sometimes enhance the compositional structure of an image.

Using image-editing software, contrast can be adjusted with the contrast slider in the Brightness and Contrast adjustment dialog box, although this is often not the best way to achieve the effect. The contrast slider can push pixel values through the black and white limits, producing shadows with little detail or blown-out highlights. These effects are called 'clipping'. The Level or Curves adjustment is better. With Levels or Curves, the black and white points of the image are pinned and the contrast curve can be adjusted either through multiple points (Curves) or by moving a central point (the grey or gamma point slider in Levels). The Greek letter gamma was originally the value used to describe the slope of the contrast curve in film.

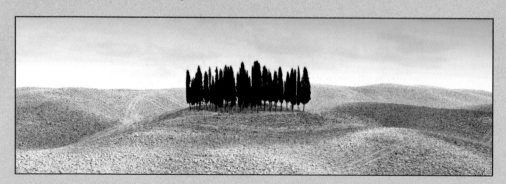

Toscano (above)

The high-contrast approach helps emphasise the graphic qualities in this symmetrical panoramic composition of a Tuscan landscape.

Photographer: Ilona Wellmann.

Technical summary: Four frames taken with a Nikon Coolpix 5700, 1/500 sec at f5.1, merged and sepia-toned in Photoshop.

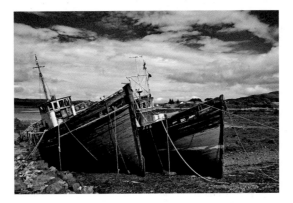

High contrast

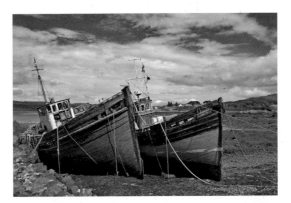

Normal contrast

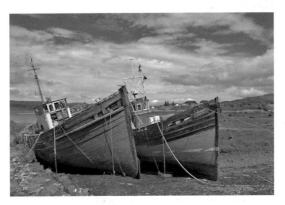

Low contrast

'The artist must feel free to select his rendering of tonality as he is to express any other aspect of the subject.'
Ansel Adams (landscape photographer)

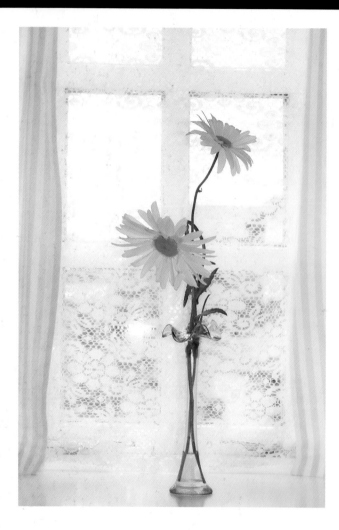

Windowsill (left)

Colour can be given high-key treatment as effectively as black-and-white. Flooded with natural backlight in a well-lit window these flowers were perfect for a high-key approach. On-camera flash was used to lift the flower blooms. Although there was plenty of bright ambient light reflecting around the deep, white-painted window recess, it was not enough to show the subject crisply. Flash compensation of -1 stop reduced the flash component of the image for balance. Trial exposures were assessed using the camera histogram display to avoid lost highlights.

Photographer: David Präkel.

Technical summary: Nikon D100 with 60mm Micro-Nikkor, 1/180 sec at f8, background slightly desaturated in Photoshop.

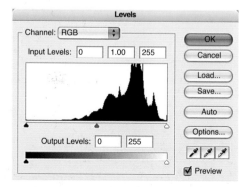

High-key effects

A true high-key composition will contain a full range of tones from black to white, but will have a preponderance of lighter tones.

A high-key image is not the same as an overexposed image, which will not have any dark tones whatever. In portraits, pupils and shadows in the nostrils or ear tend to be the only black parts in an otherwise light-toned image.

Some subjects – snow scenes and young children, in particular – would be perfect subjects for a high-key treatment. Great care is needed lighting high-key images as it is easy to overexpose the image. This is much more of a problem with digital cameras. The photographer must decide whether a tone

is required in the 'whites' or whether the white will be 'blown out', which means the printing paper shows through in these areas. Studio high-key images invariably use white backgrounds and plenty of light is required to create the effect.

When taking light-meter readings from high-key subjects it is important to use an incident light meter or to use substitute metering from a standard grey card. Incident (hand-held) light meters record the light falling on the subject – rather than the light reflected from the subject – as does a conventional meter in the camera. Taking a reflected light meter reading without using exposure compensation would produce a grey rather than a white image.

A correctly exposed high-key image of largely white objects. The digital histogram (see opposite) shows few mid-grey tones and a predominance of light greys.

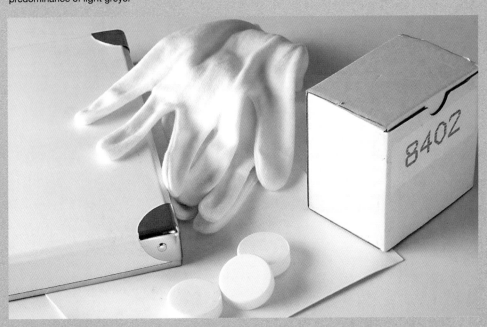

Low-key effects

True low-key images retain a full range of tones from black to pure white, but they are composed mainly of darker tones. They should be thought of as predominantly dark images with a small area of high contrast.

Low-key images have a sombre, moody feel and can be produced in one of two ways. A composition containing only dark elements when correctly exposed will produce a low-key image. Alternatively, a scene with a normal range of tones can be darkened right down and lit selectively to produce a low-key image, too. In the studio, it is usual to use non-reflecting black material (velvet will look blacker than black paper) and high-contrast lighting to achieve the low-key effect. Underexposing a normal scene will not produce the same effect as a low-key image, as the image will have no highlight information at all.

One difficulty with low-key images is holding on to shadow detail. If you are using a light meter, don't use a reflected light meter for images of this kind unless you meter from an 18-percent reflectance standard grey card. If you use a reflected meter reading without exposure compensation, the image will not be dark enough. A reflected light meter tends to underexpose dark and overexpose light subjects. Instead, use an incident light meter to get an accurate exposure for low-key as well as high-key images. An incident light meter that measures the light falling on the subject will achieve a correct exposure.

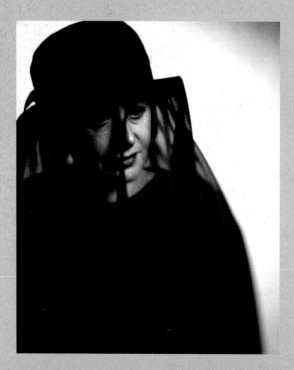

Portrait of Spring Hurlburt (left)

This low-key studio portrait of a woman in veil and hat evokes a sense of sadness and mourning. The picture was taken of the subject after her father's death and she contributed the image to the photographer's project 'Different Hats'. The left side of the subject's face bears the lightest tones and shows good modelling from the key light – the natural skin tones are darkened by the veil. The dark upper-right corner of the print 'holds the subject in' and emphasises her gaze at a close-by but invisible point out of the frame.

Photographer: Jim Allen.

Technical summary: Sinar P 5 x 4 large-format camera, 210mm Nikkor f5.6, scanned from Polaroid Type 54.

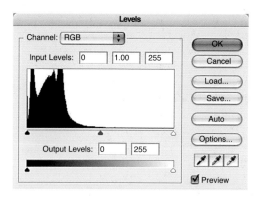

A correctly exposed low-key image of black objects (below). The digital histogram, left, correctly displays no information above mid-grey and a predominance of dark greys and shadows.

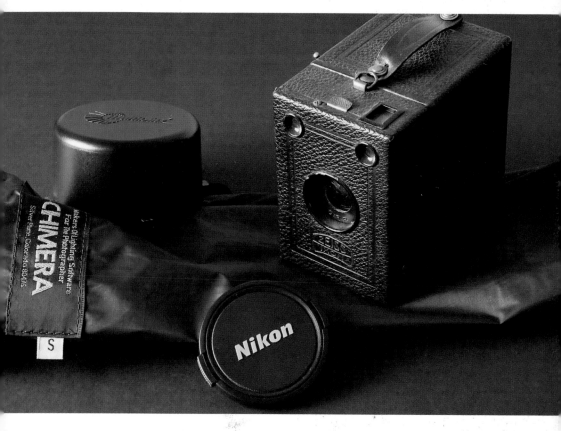

Colour

Photographers deal with light. Without light, there are no colours. Pure, white light is an equal addition of red, green, and blue light – these are called 'additive primaries'. 'Primary colours' are the colours from which all other colours can be made. Taking away each of the additive primaries from white light creates in turn cyan (white less red), magenta (white less green) and yellow (white less blue) light, which are known as the 'subtractive primaries'.

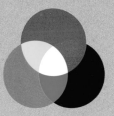 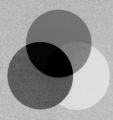

The additive and subtractive primaries.

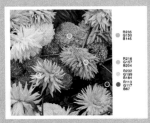

RGB values

Computer simulation of colour is achieved by mixing red, green and blue light on an integer scale from 0 to 255. With 256 levels (8-bits) per channel, this model represents 16.7 million colours. A colour can be described by the three values of its RGB components: for example, a very warm red might be red 218, green 63, blue 53.

Our eyes, computer monitors and digital camera sensors all work with the red, green and blue components of white light. The eye has sensors for each of these colours, just as the digital camera chip has these colours in a mosaic over its surface. (Digital cameras use twice as many green pixels as blue or red to match human sensitivity to green light.)

Colour wheel

Photographers find it useful to represent colour on a wheel (see below). Imagine an equal-sided triangle with each of the three points labelled red, green, blue (RGB) in any order. Now imagine a second triangle upside-down on top of the first. The points on that triangle will be labelled with the subtractive primary colours: yellow as a mix of red and green, cyan as a mix of green and blue and magenta as a mix of red and blue. Imagine each spot of pure colour blending into the next to create the colour wheel. (Hue or hue shift is described in degrees, which represents an angular shift in colour around the colour wheel.)

  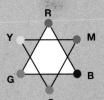 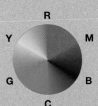

The colour wheel can be used for both technical and aesthetic considerations. Technically, it is used to work out colour corrections (adding the diametrically opposite colour to correct an unwanted colour cast). It is also useful when working out which colour filter is needed with monochromatic film to darken and lighten the appearance of certain colours in the finished print. Blue/cyan skies are darkened by using a yellow, orange or red filter. Yellow-green foliage is lightened on black-and-white film by using a yellow-green filter. The colour wheel rule for filters is that opposite colours darken while similar colours lighten.

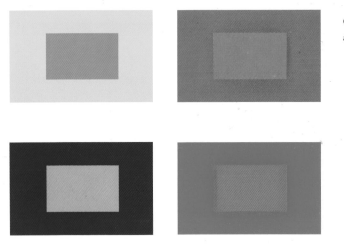

Colour in harmony (left) and discord (right).

In aesthetic terms, colours adjacent to each other on the colour wheel are described as being in 'harmony', whereas colours opposite to each other are said to be in 'discord'. A blue flower stands out from a yellow background or a red sailboat stands out on a sea reflecting a blue sky. 'Warm' colours revolve around yellow and 'cold' colours around blue. Colour contrast comes from different colours of the same brightness or the same saturation. Hues far apart on the colour wheel show a great contrast, but those diametrically opposite show the greatest contrast.

Colour associations
Colours also have psychological associations (though this is very culturally dependent). In Western culture, red is a signal colour associated with warning, action, fire and anger. Not surprisingly, red is heavily used in advertising. White is associated with purity – but in the East it is connected to death and mourning. Blue is associated with cold, clarity, space and winter. Yellow, the colour of the sun, is associated with heat, life, joy and summer. For the psychologist, green is a 'reserved' colour and considered to be neither warm nor cold, active nor passive. It is associated with nature, serenity and security. However, 'acid' green is a great photographic attention-grabber. Brown – the earth colour – signifies warmth, peace and harmony.

Colour temperature

If a block of iron is heated it passes through all the colours of red, orange and yellow, from dull red to white hot, at which point the iron burns (oxidises). The real temperature of the object can even be estimated from its colour. Colour temperature relates back to this concept as all our light sources are radiating energy. Colour temperature is measured in Kelvin (K).

Light source	Colour temperature	Colour
Candles and oil lamps	1800–2000K	Rich yellow-orange
Household light bulbs	2800–3000K	Yellow
Sunrise or sunset	4000–4500K	Rich golden
Morning/evening sunshine	5000K	Yellow-white
Noon daylight/electronic flash	5500–6500K	White
Hazy sky	6000–7000K	Blue-white
Heavily overcast sky	7500K	Quite blue
Reflections from clear blue sky in shade	16000K	Very blue

The quality (temperature) of the illuminating light needs to be considered when you take colour pictures. The time of day has a big effect on the colour of light. Reflected light takes the colour of the surface from which it reflects.

Colour temperature can be adjusted by choosing from a range of blue- and amber-coloured filters over the lens. These filters do not have to be used to correct light for pure white, but can be used to artificially warm up or cool down an image. On digital cameras colour temperature is adjusted either on fixed settings through the White Balance menu or by entering a colour temperature in Kelvin. The Daylight setting for White Balance on a digital camera or 'daylight' film interprets 'daylight' as the sun in a blue sky, one-third filled with fluffy, white clouds (the sun shining in a clear, blue sky is actually too blue).

Achromatic colours

Some of the most important colours in colour photography are the so-called achromatic or 'without colour' colours – black, grey and white. These act as a foil for the colours of your composition. Any colour cast present in the scene will show first in these colours. White becomes grey as brightness is changed. A yellow cast is warm, while a shift to blue is cold. (See also the section on Warmtone and cooltone, page 90.)

Spot colour

Small patches of very intense colour can be used to dramatic effect.

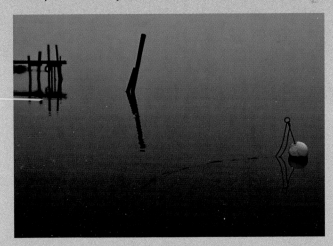

Red in fog (left)

The single spot of red colour of the buoy floating in a lake reflecting grey (achromatic background) boosts the graphic impact of the composition.

Photographer:
Trine Sirnes Thorne.

Technical summary: Nikon Coolpix 880.

Chromatic colours

The strongest, most intense, or highly saturated colours can confuse and dazzle the viewer or more simply attract their attention.

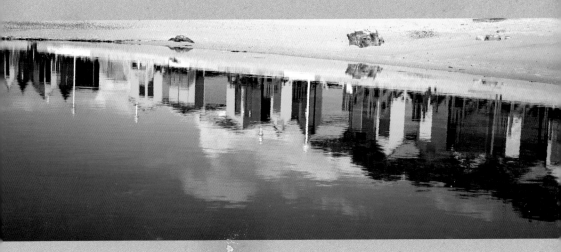

St. James beach huts (above)

Long row of beach huts painted in primary colours near Cape Town, South Africa. The reflection of the strand and water's edge add a twist to this colourful panorama.

Photographer: John Barclay.

Technical summary: Hasselblad XPan with 90mm lens, 1/60 sec at f8, Fuji Velvia 50.

Saturation

Saturation is a technical term meaning strength of colour. Neutral grey has no colour saturation. A bowl of fruit with ripe red apples and yellow bananas features highly saturated colours.

A meadow in morning haze will show only soft, pastel (unsaturated) colours. In compositional terms, colour saturation communicates an intensity of mood or feeling and acts like a volume control on any basic colour association.

In low light, only the strongest colours preserve their intensity. In very bright light – glare – the colours appear washed out. In strongly backlit scenes colours can contrast with deep, black shadows, while flat, bright light creates the most saturated colours.

To desaturate an image in-camera, use a diffusion or fog filter. Even something as simple as a plastic bag or nylon gauze pulled over the lens produces a degree of desaturation. It is harder to increase saturation. The so-called 'extra colour' negative and transparency films offer a degree of colour boost.

Digital cameras can provide an option to choose a saturated or desaturated image, though it is often better to delay your options and achieve the effect later using computer software. Colour-enhancing filters 'pop', or boost, one wavelength of light – a 'redhancer', for example, will pop reds. These filters, made of rare earth glass, are often used to enrich the mood of garden images taken in autumn and can be used with digital or with film cameras.

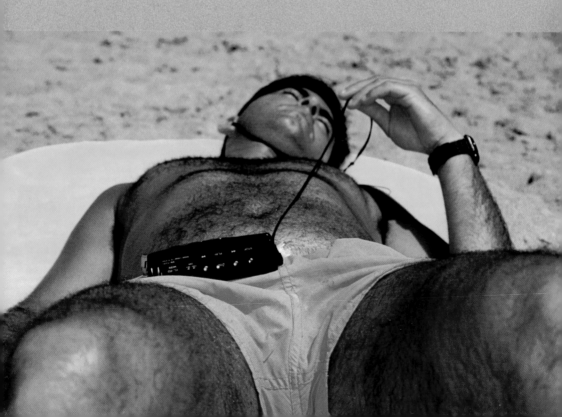

Computer modelling

Computers give digital photographers control over the separate colour and luminance components of an image. One method is via the HSL colour model. This describes colour in terms of its hue (colour), saturation (strength) and lightness (whiteness or the degree to which it appears to reflect light). This model enables digital photographers to make changes in composition after the taking by altering the colour of certain elements, and increasing or decreasing the saturation of colours.

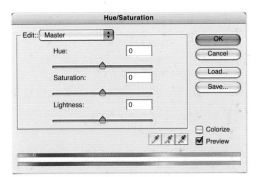

Adobe Photoshop Hue/Saturation Lightness adjustment.

Benidorm, Spain, 1997 (facing opposite)

Parr achieved the rich 'seaside' intensity of colour by combining ring flash (flash around and on axis of the lens) with the super-saturated Agfa Ultra colour negative film.

Photographer:

Martin Parr.

Technical summary:

None provided.

Kippford (below)

Desaturating enhances the pastel tones of these cottages in Kippford, Scotland, but to keep some strength in the tractor, a bitmap (black-and-white only) version of the image has been layered in. Some image-retouching was performed to simplify the skyline.

Photographer: David Präkel.

Technical summary: Nikon D100 with 18–35mm zoom, 1/320sec at f9.5 with +1 EV compensation.

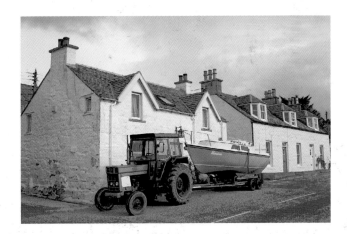

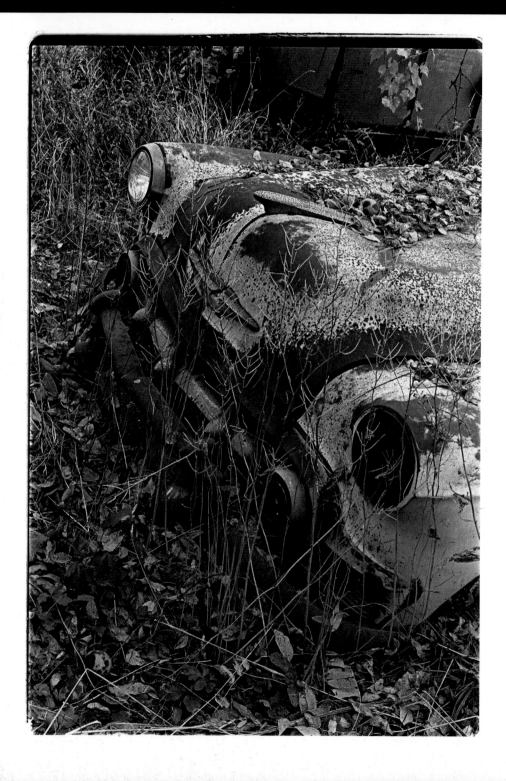

Limited palette

Reducing the number of colours in an image can simplify and strengthen the composition. Artists working in oil paints mix their colours on a palette. For photographers, an image with a 'limited palette' is one that uses only a few shades of one colour. This may extend to a small group of colours closely associated with the colour – at most there will be two small clusters of colour in an image described as having a limited palette.

In landscape photography, where the photographer has least control, changes in weather can produce the best conditions. Mist, fog and rain all reduce the palette of colour, thereby simplifying the subject matter. By moving in closer to the subject and looking more at detail, the range of tones and contrasts in colour can also be reduced.

Ultimate control over the palette of colours in your images can be achieved by taking your pictures in black and white and then hand-colouring them. This is either achieved with oils or washes on silver gelatin prints made on fibre paper or on the computer. Marshall oils and oil pencils are probably the best-known products for true hand-colouring. Specialist suppliers still stock felt-tip and brush-tip photo dye pens; alternatively, bottled dyes and retouching kits are available and the dyes applied diluted with a brush.

The image-manipulation technique is to scan a greyscale image and convert the image space to RGB. Using selected colours from the Color Picker or, better still, sampled colours from other images, you paint these colours into the image using a range of soft-edge brushes on layers with the blending mode set to Soft Light or Color. Adjusting the opacity of the brush or layer introduces more subtle effects. Keeping each colour on separate layers enables you to adjust the hues of the colour palette on each individual layer.

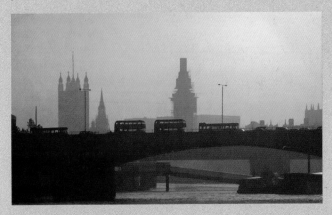

Waterloo Bridge, London (left)

A misty evening light and a telephoto lens limit the palette of colours in this atmospheric scene on the River Thames.

Photographer: David Präkel.

Technical summary: Leica R4, 180mm Elmarit, Ektachrome 100.

Hand-coloured car (facing opposite)

A digital hand-coloured image of an abandoned station wagon on a ruined farmstead, Ovid, New York. Colours for this image were sampled from a second image of fallen leaves.

Photographer: David Präkel.

Technical summary: Leica R4 with 35–70mm Vario-Elmar zoom, Kodak TMax 400 black-and-white film plus colour sampled from second image on Elitechrome Extra Colour film.

Black and white

For many years black-and-white film was the only acceptable medium for fine-art photography. Colour images were regarded with suspicion as something of a novelty until William Eggleston's groundbreaking exhibition at the Museum of Modern Art in New York in the early 1970s.

While colour has its place, black and white still represents the ultimate in photographic abstraction. Black-and-white images are not just colour images with the colour drained from them; they represent tonality, shape and texture more explicitly. Black-and-white photography is about the presence or absence of light and its creation of texture and form.

We do not see in black and white, so predicting the look of a black-and-white image is largely a matter of experience. Screwing up the eyes and squinting reduces their colour performance to some small extent, which can help with pre-visualisation.

The way in which monochromatic film responds to different wavelengths of light – different colours, in other words – gives it its characteristic look. For many photographers film has a unique, inimitable quality. Film's sensitivity to colour can be manipulated by using coloured filters over the camera lens: filters of a similar colour to the subject lighten, opposite colours darken. On black-and-white film, for example, a yellow, orange or red filter would darken a cyan/blue sky, while a yellow-green filter would lighten foliage.

Digital black and white is becoming increasingly popular, although the image is always originated in colour and converted to black and white using software. The practice of shooting black-and-white film can be a great help in visualising tonal relationships and in seeking out subjects worthy of monochromatic presentation. Black-and-white photography offers a compositional discipline that will improve all other forms of image-making.

'When you photograph people in color, you are photographing their clothes. When you photograph them in black and white, you photograph their souls.'

Ted Grant (Canadian photographer)

Foggy evening (facing opposite)

There is nothing that colour could add to this image and much it would take away. Form, scale and shape are all made abstract and enhanced by careful subject selection and the use of black and white.

Photographer: Ilona Wellmann.

Technical summary: Nikon Coolpix 5700, 1/250 sec at f5.0 using the black-and-white mode, contrast and levels were adjusted and the image sepia-toned in Photoshop.

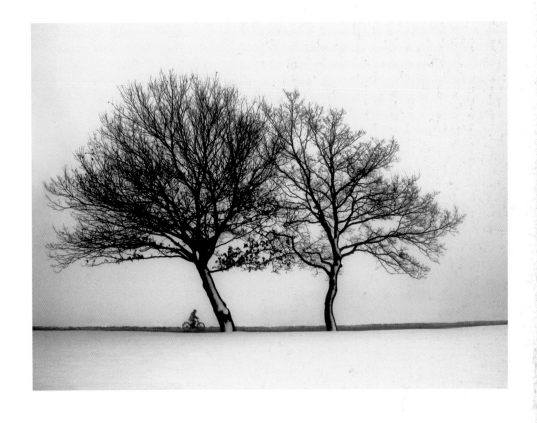

Warmtone and cooltone

Toning black-and-white pictures was originally introduced to preserve them, but there are also aesthetic reasons for chemical toning or the digital equivalent.

With silver-halide based images the silver salt is chemically altered by toning to produce a range of brown- or blue-toned images – perhaps the best-known toning process being sepia. Alternatively, the silver can be substituted or augmented by another metal, such as selenium. This produces a range of potential greys from graphite to a rich purple grey, depending on how long the print is left in the toner. Toning with gold, copper, iron and chrome have all been popular in the past – at least with photographers, if not with health-and-safety experts. In a fully toned image all the blacks and greys will turn to shades of brown; in a split-tone image the lighter parts of the image are brown but the darker tone is more the original black. Split-toning using sepia and selenium is possible and has particular appeal.

All these chemical effects have a characteristic look that can be duplicated with image-editing software for digital images. Selective toning of black-and-white paper prints can be a very hit-and-miss affair. Colour is laid down on selected parts of the subject only – one leaf from a carpet of leaves, for example. This treatment is so much easier to achieve digitally, without the need for careful applications of fast-acting chemical or elaborate masks laid with rubdown sheet or painted on as liquids.

Black-and-white photo papers come in a range of tones, varying from brown-yellow blacks to blue blacks. The brown end of the scale is referred to as 'warmtone', while the blue end of the scale is called 'cooltone' or 'coldtone'. Again, these distinct looks can be achieved digitally.

Warmtone and cooltone effects.

Cooltone (bluish)　　< Neutral grey >　　Warmtone (brownish)

Underground (facing opposite)

Image of the London Underground that uses the 'language' of warm and cold tones to contrast the cold-blue corridor of the tube station with its warm, yellow depths.

Photographer: Tom McGhee, Trevillion Images.

Technical summary: Nikon F5 with Nikon 20mm lens, exposure unrecorded, colour negative film was cross-processed in E6 chemistry.

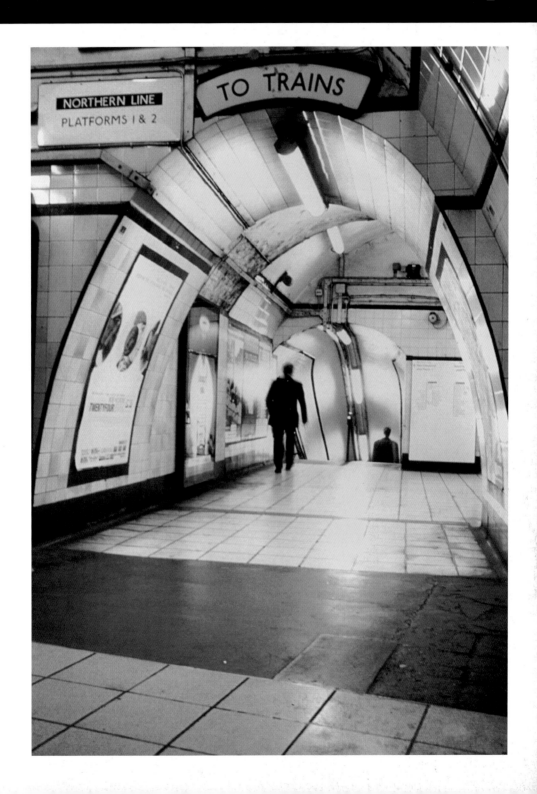

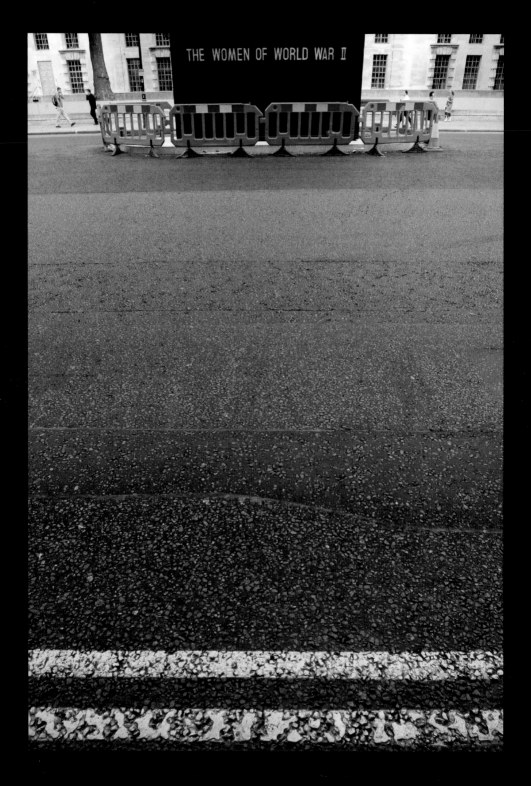

THE WOMEN OF WORLD WAR II

Composition is a process of organising space. **All photographic imaging starts with selection, but before the photographer even thinks about a subject, he or she must give consideration to the proportions of the frame that will contain it. There are various film and digital formats and a choice of aspect ratios for frames. The frame of the image can be horizontal (landscape), vertical (portrait), square or panoramic, the latter offering the photographer a particular challenge with composition.**

Having selected a subject, the photographer needs to know where the subject is best placed in the frame and how big it should be – as both position and size have a major influence on how the viewer will read the image. The advantages of composing images in the camera over cropping later in image-manipulation software are many. Composing in advance requires mor skill and creativity. The photographer must look at both the balance of all the formal elements and the foreground-to-background balance. We'll look at the problems of symmetry and the pitfalls of the perfectly balanced image – in addition to related notions of symmetry, beauty and the human face – in more detail in the next few pages.

Selective focus and the use of lens aperture is another aspect of the compositional process for consideration as they give photographers control over which part of their image appears in sharp focus – a feature unique to photography. Sharpness, by convention, signifies the importance of the subject. Again, we'll look in more detail at focus, the quality of out-of-focus areas of the image and the use of depth of field and hyperfocal focusing to maximise sharpness.

Cityscape (facing opposite)
In his cityscape images Zafeiris says he is trying to capture the 'unseen'. This image at first presents a void between the near barrier of the yellow parking lines and the distant monument and its temporary red plastic fence. These elements 'hold open' a space that only on further investigation reveals intriguing textures.

Photographer: Sotiris Zafeiris.

Technical summary: Canon EOS D60, Sigma 15–30mm zoom lens, 1/90 sec at f5.6, ISO 200.

Frames

Framing a section of the world to create an image is arguably the most important part of the process of composition. The proportions and orientation of the frame (horizontal or vertical) dictate how the process of composition proceeds. Each format has its own 'sweet spots' in the frame that demand a different approach in terms of subject placement.

Rectangular photographs are commonplace, though this has not always been the case. Early Kodak cameras created a circular image, which is logical as lenses project circular and not rectangular images.

Frames can, of course, be any shape. The proportions of rectangular frames – their 'aspect ratios' – differ depending on whether the image was captured digitally or on film.

The 'aspect ratio' of an image is its width divided by its height, which is more often written as two whole numbers e.g. 3:2 (35mm format: 36mm [width] x 24mm [height]). Referring back to the Golden Mean, or Section (see page 22), the ideal would be a rectangle of 1:1.618 proportions. The table shows how digital and film formats measure up – the older 6 x 9cm format, digital SLRs and 35mm come closest to this notion of the 'ideal'.

Film type	Aspect ratio	Image
Large-format film		
5 x 4in and 10 x 8in	1.25	7
Medium-format roll film		
6 x 17cm Panoramic	2.833	
6 x 12cm Panoramic	2.0	
6 x 9cm	1.5	6
6 x 8cm	1.333	
6 x 7cm	1.286	4
6 x 6cm	1.0	3
6 x 4.5cm	1.333	5
35mm miniature film		
24 x 36mm 3:2	1.5	1
24 x 65mm Hasselblad XPan	2.708	2
Digital		
Digital SLRs	1.5	
Compact cameras and Four-thirds (4:3) digital cameras	1.333	

Sailing boat (facing opposite)

This sequence shows how different film formats would capture and crop the same scene if it were taken with a range of cameras (with a standard focal-length lens) from the same viewpoint.

Photographer: David Präkel.

Technical summary: Various formats (above) and exposure settings.

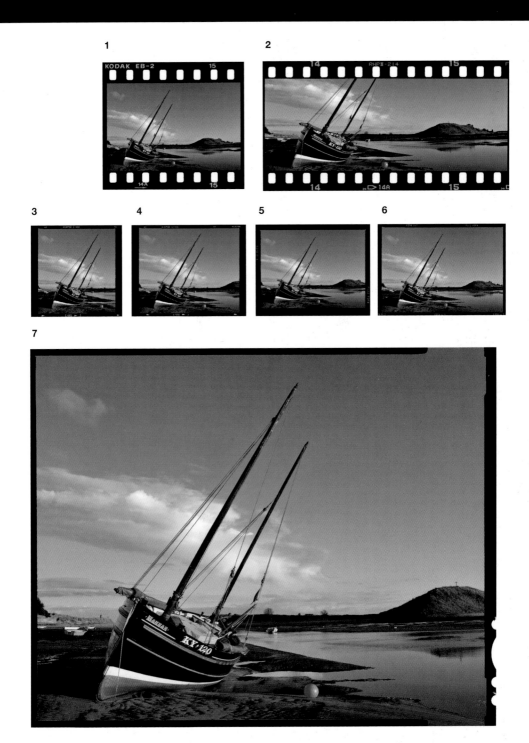

The different formats.

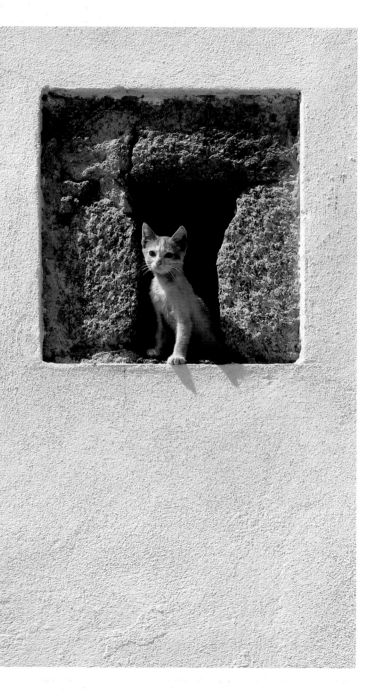

Location in the frame

It is important to think about the shape of the chosen subject and to judge how the subject can be visually separated from the 'field' or background. There is a natural tendency among novices to place the subject centrally within the frame, with a little breathing space between it and the top and bottom of the frame – known as 'bull's eye syndrome'. With most formats, this position leaves two large redundant areas at either side of the subject. This framing has an almost magnetic quality and, at first, it becomes a hard fight not to frame all subjects in this way. There are times when it is appropriate – see the section on symmetry (page 114) – but the visual argument has to be compelling.

Trying consciously to move the subject off-centre towards one of the four corners of the frame begins to free up the composition. A more radical solution might be to crop the subject so it is only partially present in the frame. Geometric considerations such as dynamic symmetry can help, but the where and why will be dictated by the subject.

Depending on the subject, it will lay claim to part of the space around it. In the expectation of its moving off, a car will 'own' the space in front of it – similarly, an empty chair. Objects also tend to dominate the space over which their shadow falls. In portraiture, it is essential to consider the space in front of and behind the head, especially with profiles, as the effect created by the two positions can be dramatically different.

With some photographic genres, it is difficult to break down the image clearly between subject/field. In landscape photography, for example, the subject *is* the field, although care still must be taken with the placement of key elements.

1   2   3   4

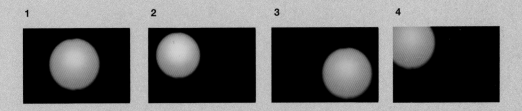

Where in the frame? 1 Symmetrical and static; 2 Offset to top left, which creates some tension; 3 Offset to bottom right, which creates little dynamic or tension; 4 Offset to top left and cropped, which is more dynamic and provides 'closure'.

Window to the world (facing opposite)

The cat has room to leap – the position of the cat up the frame increases tension, stressed by the low viewpoint. There are three embedded frames with the centre of interest (the cat's head) placed at one of the four strongest focal points in the main image frame.

Photographer: Jorge Coimbra.

Technical summary: Canon Powershot G3, 1/500 sec at f8, ISO 50.

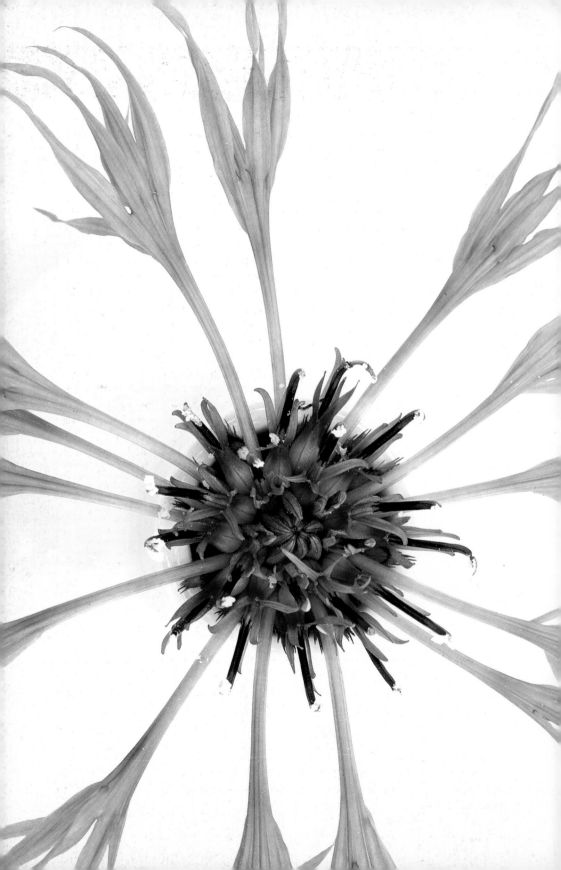

Size in the frame

In addition to its place in the frame, think about the relative size of the subject to its field. What do you want to say about your subject and its location? Do you want the subject to dominate the frame or merge with the background? If your subject is a flower bursting with colour and energy, maximise it so that it bursts out of the frame.

Just as there is a mesmeric attraction to placing a subject in the centre of the frame, we have also a natural reluctance to crop. Timidly nibbling at the edges of a subject produces weak images. Important detail must be retained, but the brain will rapidly complete what has been cropped out, especially with geometric or common forms. Newspapers rarely publish a head and shoulders portrait without cropping through the forehead. This gives more prominence on the page to the face. Ideally, cropping is performed in-camera as this gives the best-quality full-frame enlargement.

Exaggeration is one of the photographer's most powerful tools. Cropping a subject tightly for maximum detail and impact is one such example. If appropriate to the subject, show the subject as small as possible in the frame – just large enough to be recognisable. Put a camera in the hands of a child and they appreciate and explore these extremes with little regard for convention, and it is worth putting it aside with your own photography to explore the limits. Further ideas can be found in the section on Scale (see page 34).

Moving the camera relative to the subject and changing the focal length of the lens alters the relationship between subject and background, as shown in the section on Perspective (see page 28). Alternatively, if you want to crop an image, don't move the position of the camera, but use different focal-length settings on a zoom lens to achieve different crops.

1 2 3 4

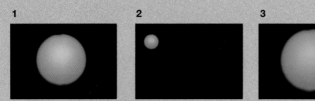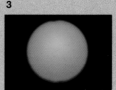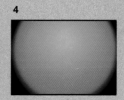

What size in the frame? 1 Symmetrical, with redundant space to the left and right; 2 Small, but still recognisable subject embedded in its environment, which is more interesting; 3 Symmetrical, frame-filling subject becomes uncomfortably close to the top and bottom of the edges of the frame; 4 Finally, a strong crop around the subject retains its identity, but also packs the frame with detail.

Cornflower (facing opposite)

This cornflower is intentionally overexposed by 1 stop to lose all but the faintest trace of the white circular vase. Exuberant, frame-filling detail – two petals remain to show what has been cropped elsewhere.

Photographer: David Präkel.

Technical summary: Nikon D100, 60mm Micro-Nikkor, 1/3sec at f22, natural light with wrap-around reflector.

Composition in-camera

It is a good discipline to give as much consideration to the film or sensor area as possible when creating the image. This is called in-camera composition. Full-frame images make the best-quality enlargements.

It is far easier to compose in-camera when the camera viewing/focusing system is an image projected onto a ground-glass screen that the photographer views directly. This puts you at one remove from the real world and begins to produce the look of the final two-dimensional image. Medium- and large-format cameras work this way, and many

also invert or flip the image (depending on the type of camera). This can be hard to get used to or just another stage in the process of abstraction, depending on your point of view, but many photographers prefer this method for composing images.

The SLR (single-lens-reflex) camera presents a view that is close to the final image, because you are looking through the picture-taking lens. This is especially true if the camera has a depth-of-field preview button and the effect of the taking aperture can also be assessed. The effects of filters over the lens also show.

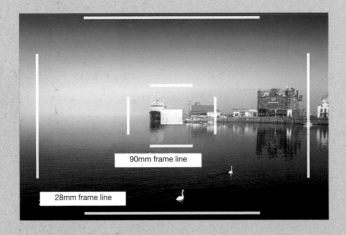

90mm frame line

28mm frame line

The extended view of the viewfinder or rangefinder camera can help plan the shot.

In comparison to SLRs, viewfinder or rangefinder cameras can only show the effect of alternative lenses as frames within an overall fixed view. You are also not able to judge the effect of depth of field. If the viewfinder is set some distance away from the taking lens on the camera body it will not frame exactly the same view – the closer the camera gets to the subject the worse this effect, or 'parallax', becomes. However, the view/rangefinder camera has one major advantage over other viewing systems in that it shows what exists or is occurring outside the frame. This enables the photographer to track compositional elements as they come into frame. Cartier-Bresson was a master of this form of composition and spent his entire working life using Leica rangefinder cameras for this reason (see opposite). His images are often reproduced with the black frame border, which emphasises their composition in-camera.

'To me, photography is the simultaneous recognition, in a fraction of a second, of the significance of an event as well as of a precise organisation of forms which give that event its proper expression.'

Henri Cartier-Bresson (photographer and painter)

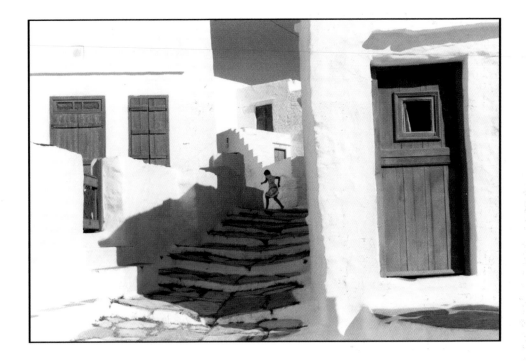

Siphos, Greece, 1961 (above)

Everything comes together in the viewfinder frame at the 'decisive moment'. Form, tone, space, line and texture is balanced, waiting only for the 'actor' to take centre stage.

Photographer: Henri Cartier-Bresson.

Technical summary: None provided.

Horizontal format

The horizontal rectangular frame is known as 'landscape' format because landscape is the subject with which this format is most strongly associated. As a shape, the horizontal rectangle lends an image a sense of stability and direction. The landscape format emphasises the horizon and any part of a horizontal line or plane in the image. It encourages broad vistas, especially when the proportions of the frame extend beyond the accepted classical proportions.

Taking portraits in the horizontal format leaves potentially redundant areas on either side of the subject. The face will also be smaller in the frame than if the composition were in 'portrait' format. However, moving the subject to one side of the frame opens up background detail (in or out of focus) that can provide interesting context.

The horizontal format offers greater opportunity to include space in front of or behind the subject's head and can be used to increase a sense of alienation, for example, if the face is placed near a corner or edge and appears to be moving out of the frame.

The vertical centreline of the horizontal frame always seems to be a compositionally 'dangerous' place to split an image. The exact centreline becomes an axis that challenges the viewer to compare the make-up of the two halves. In the hands of a master such as Henri Cartier-Bresson, whose photography was very much influenced by his compositional studies as a painter, this usage can provide a strong fulcrum about which the image turns. But there must be a thoroughgoing composition or the picture will end up simply having two halves.

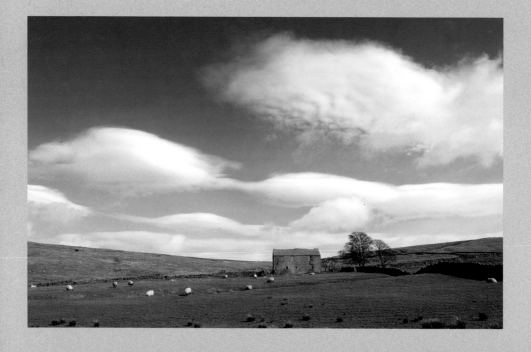

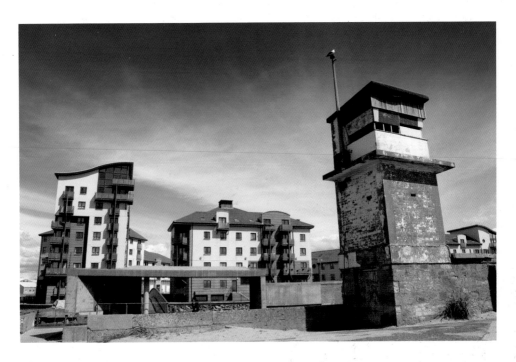

New building development in docks at Ayr, Scotland (above)

The low viewpoint and strongly converging verticals from the wide-angle lens stress the verticality of the development, even in this horizontal composition.

Photographer: David Präkel.

Technical summary: Nikon D100 with 18–35mm zoom, 1/750sec at f9.5.

Carrshield (facing opposite)

The low horizon and farm building just tucked into the dip in the hills in the background serves to emphasise the sky.

Photographer: David Präkel.

Technical summary: Nikon D100 with 18–35mm zoom, 1/400sec at f11.

Vertical format

The vertical rectangular frame is called the 'portrait' format because it comfortably encompasses head-and-shoulder style portraits. The vertical format emphasises any vertical line or plane. It also exaggerates foreground-to-background depth in the picture. For this reason alone, images of urban landscape are often composed in vertical format to emphasise the 'concrete canyons' of a city.

The vertical format makes for more dramatic diagonals than the landscape format as the angles within the frame can be steeper. When the subject is a landscape, the vertical format can be used to emphasise a gorge or rocky outcrop, especially when coupled with a high viewpoint. With its exaggeration of depth, the vertical frame is ideally suited to large-format images full of extensive, sharp detail, from the flowers in the foreground to distant hills – hyperfocal focusing and a camera with a tilting back are essential.

Formats with a wide aspect ratio can look unstable when turned to the vertical. Panoramic formats in particular require great care when used vertically, although, with appropriate subjects they can produce dramatic images that appear to tower over the viewer.

The vertical format is also ideal for the standing human form. If a standing person is photographed full-length on 35mm film in 'landscape' format there is really not enough detail in the face, as the image is physically too small on the negative. The portrait format can comfortably and elegantly encompass gestures and movement.

The vertical format is also very commercial, since it is often used for full-page illustrations in books and magazines, which themselves tend to follow this format. At one time, Fuji launched a 6 x 8cm format camera specifically to match the widespread magazine front cover format to avoid the need for image cropping.

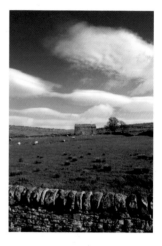

Carrshield (above)

The vertical format provides an opportunity to include the foreground drystone wall. Hyperfocal focusing is important to retain sharp front to back detail. The centrally placed horizon reduces the impact of the sky somewhat.

Photographer: David Präkel.

Technical summary: Nikon D100 with 18–35mm zoom, 1/250 sec at f11.

**New building development
in docks at Ayr, Scotland
(right)**

Moving closer to the old
dock lookout required a
slightly higher viewpoint
to keep the converging
verticals within acceptable
limits. There is a much
greater sense of foreground
and background, of the
old and new. Angled tiles
give additional interest to
the foreground.

Photographer: David Präkel.

Technical summary: Nikon D100
with 18–35mm zoom, 1/500 sec
at f11.

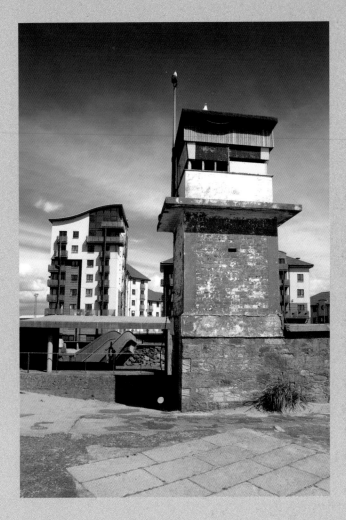

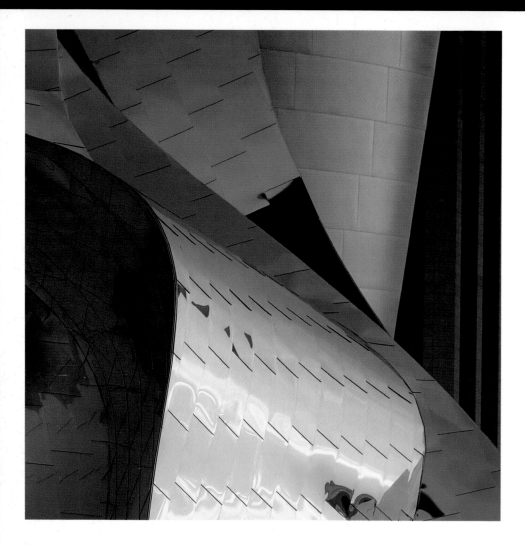

Walt Disney concert hall (above)

The square format can barely contain the massive forms and textures of the roof of the Frank Gehry-designed concert hall in downtown Los Angeles.

Photographer: Brad Kim.

Technical summary: Canon EOS 10D with Canon EF 85mm f1.8 USM, aperture-priority exposure at f22 with -0.5 stop EV compensation, ISO 100.

Square format

With the exception of some of the Polaroid instant films, the only square format currently available is the 6 x 6cm image on medium-format roll film. Working with this format has one major advantage – you never have to turn the camera on its side. Yet, the disadvantage is temptation to compose either horizontally or vertically within its confines and to crop when printing. This approach either disregards or misunderstands the quality advantage of the greater film area; the shot might as well have been taken on 645 format. Square images can, of course, be created later by cropping other formats, but the resulting images may not be as rigorously composed as those formatted to a square in-camera.

Square images are symmetrical about both the horizontal and vertical axes, which lends solidity and stability. The resulting quarters are also squares, and the whole form is strongly directed around the centre, which can lack dynamism. The diagonals, however, can be used to dramatic compositional effect.

Where the subject is appropriate, the square can be a rewarding format. In some fields – plant and flower photography, for instance – the square works well, offering big, symmetrically placed and tightly cropped images, although it is a challenge to avoid composing something repetitive and stereotypical.

For the landscape photographer the square can create static images with very little tension, irrespective of where the horizon is placed, although with a wide-angle lens and a viewpoint that includes plenty of foreground, the square format can produce images imbued with great strength.

Having parts of the subject radically break through the square frame can add dynamism. Intentional compositional imbalances between contrasting areas, jagged lines and edges or richly curved shapes that extend beyond the visible frame can unsettle the square format and be used to great creative effect.

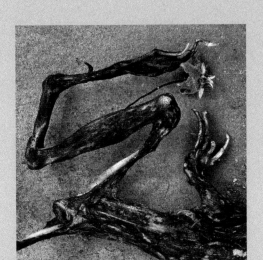

Mummified frog with dried flower of the Hoya carnosa (left)

Uncomfortable angles push against the boundaries of the severe square crop from a 5 x 4in negative.

Photographer: David Präkel.

Technical summary: Sinar F with 150mm Symmar lens, 1/8sec at f32, Ilford FP4 Plus sheet film, digital print.

Panoramic format

'Panorama' means an unobstructed view in all directions. Interestingly, some of the most dramatic panoramic images are taken, not as horizontal images, but as striking vertical compositions. This can be especially impressive with urban and industrial landscapes. It is important to compose a coherent image across the full width of any panorama and avoid leaving sections at each end of the composition that add little or nothing to it.

Despite their long history, panoramas still have a novelty value over and above the quality of their composition. Creating coherent panoramic images relies a good deal on careful location-scouting and selection of viewpoint, and the effect is often difficult to pre-visualise. The very wide format can create enough compositional problems in avoiding what widescreen filmmakers disparagingly call 'washing-line' – a composition in which smaller, self-contained images compete within the panoramic frame.

The extreme panorama, familiar to most of us from school photographs, was most likely taken with a camera using a travelling slit shutter that opened and moved to create the exposure. These and specialist rotating cameras create true panoramic images, but are often used in scientific rather than artistic or commercial applications. Horizontal 'swing' lens cameras, such as the German Noblex or the Russian Horizont, achieve extreme picture-taking angles (136–146°). Fixed lens cameras do not give quite the same coverage, but their conventional shutter avoids movement blur with the rotating lens, which captures the panorama over a specific, if short, period of time.

The relatively affordable Hasselblad XPan camera has spurred a revival in interest among film users. The XPan takes 24 x 65mm panoramas on standard 35mm film, with the added convenience of being able to switch mid-roll between the panoramic and conventionally proportioned 24 x 36mm images.

Film and digitally created panoramas are currently much in favour. Almost every digital camera is bundled with software that stitches panoramas out of a series of overlapped images, and many cameras feature 'panorama assist', which shows the appropriate overlap on the camera screen. Image-editing software enables users to 'photomerge' images taken at precise rotational angles, but rather than squaring up and cropping the resulting image, it is sometimes more interesting to leave the stepped edge, revealing where each image fits into the composite panorama.

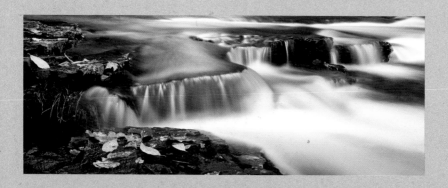

Barn door (right)

The vertical XPan format accentuates the vine reaching for the light in this study of line and colour. Essentially an outdoor still life brought to dynamic life by the choice of a wide-angle lens that gives a strong diagonal line to the lighter foreground fence, also adding depth to the image.

Photographer: John Barclay.

Technical summary: Hasselblad XPan with 90mm lens, 1 sec at f11.

Childs Falls, North-eastern Pennsylvania (facing opposite)

The sinuous line of the waterfall edge creates a strong impression as it cuts obliquely across the panoramic format. A long two-second exposure creates motion blur from water while touches of leaf colour – richly captured on highly saturated Fuji Velvia 50 film – enliven the image.

Photographer: John Barclay.

Technical summary: Hasselblad XPan with 45mm lens, hyperfocal focusing used to maximise sharpness throughout the frame.

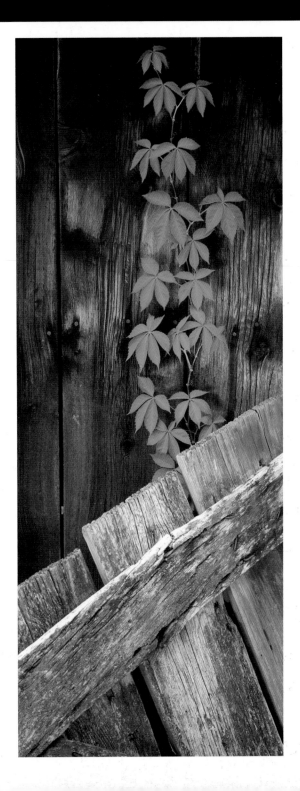

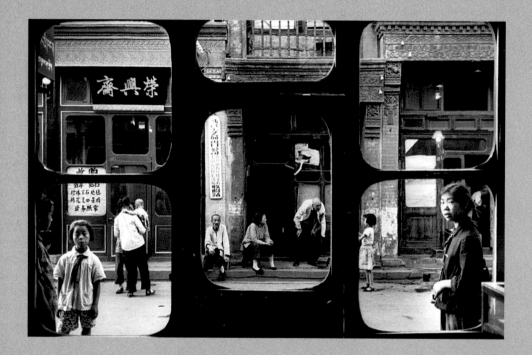

'Photography is a system of visual editing. At bottom, it is a matter of surrounding with a frame a portion of one's cone of vision, while standing in the right place at the right time.'
John Szarkowski (photography curator and critic)

Frames within frames

One of the most popular pieces of advice is to 'frame your subject'. Some photographers might be said to have made a career out of this device – for example, the self-portraits of Lee Friedlander show him framed in reflections, or even framed by picture frames hanging in a shop window. His photo essay 'The Little Screens' contains a remarkable series of images of television sets – our ultimate framing device – their light illuminating the rooms in which they are set, but the images they carry often contrast sharply with the contents of those rooms.

When we take a photograph we frame a portion of the real world. Painters create secondary framing devices within the overall frame of the canvas and photographers have also found a rich source of imagery in this technique, creating 'the image within the image'.

Taken to its extreme, the photographer can find multiple frames within an image. A good example would be of an image taken of the side of a ferryboat, revealing the disparate lives of the individuals and groups of passengers framed by the openings through the deck superstructure. Coach, bus and train windows, apartment blocks, open plan offices have all been used as vehicles for this technique.

A subject framing device in the foreground will add foreground-to-background depth in an image – overhanging tree branches are a popular device of this kind in landscape photography. This type of framing, however, unless executed sympathetically, can be little more than a visual cliché. The least attractive attempts at framing are where individual parts of branches hang into the frame like a fringe and do not seem connected to any visible tree in the image. Far better is to show the tree trunk to the side of the frame with its overhanging branches to the top.

Street in Old Beijing, 1965 (facing opposite)

Classic photographer's device of using frames from the real world – in this case, the window of an antiques shop – to create a series of disparate, but connected, images within the camera's single frame.

Photographer: Marc Riboud.

Technical summary: None provided.

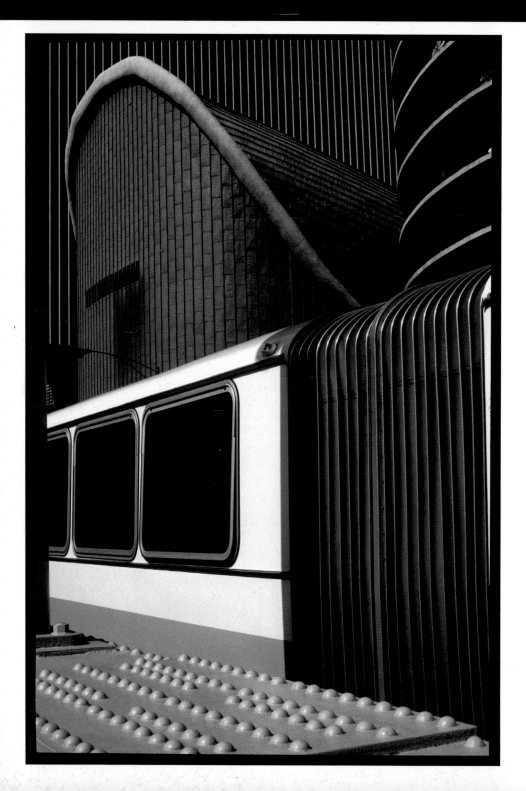

Balance

Balance is one of the main principles in design and in formal painting. The test in painting is to draw a vertical line down the centre of the image and look for a balance between the two sides. Photographers do not necessarily seek the same degree of classical harmony and may add tension to the image by shifting elements of the image to create imbalance. An image balanced by weak elements is static, while an image showing balance between strong elements is much more dynamic. The strongest sense of balance will come from the distribution of tones (light to dark) in the image. An image with a strong concentration of light or dark tone to one side of the frame, without balancing the tone, will create visual tension.

Balance does not always have to be judged about a central 'pivot'. A strong compositional element away from the centre will divide an image into two unequal parts and shift the visual pivot. 'Heavier' details such as dark tone or areas of concentrated detail will have a much stronger effect closer to the pivot point. Elements closer to the edges of the image will also gain compositional 'weight', or significance.

In addition to balancing elements from left to right of the frame, don't forget the balance of depth between foreground and background elements. More distant (therefore smaller) objects with stronger tone, colour or detail will balance less prominent (though larger) foreground objects. Images with great apparent depth will require a judgement call on the balance of three-dimensional space within the image. It is often easier to assess shapes and space by turning the print upside down or flipping a digital image vertically or laterally.

Bus form (facing opposite)

The balance in this image is provided by the articulated bus and the distinctive architecture of House of Blues and Marina City, Chicago. Circles work against rectangles, curved lines against straight lines and blocks of tone and texture about a roughly central line. There are similar textures in both foreground and background.

Photographer: David Präkel.

Technical summary: Nikon F2A with 55mm Micro-Nikkor, Kodachrome 64.

Symmetry and reflection

Symmetry is the property of an object or image in which both sides are equal but opposite about a central dividing line. Many buildings and the human body, for example, have this two-sided (bilateral) symmetry (if imperfectly in the latter case), while many flowers are radially symmetrical about any line that cuts through their centre.

Symmetrical compositions are initially very appealing and they have a strong sense of structure, although their strength is also their failing as all forces are equal and opposite. Though superficially attractive they can be too easy on the eye and lack tension.

It is a challenge to avoid centring the subject symmetrically in the frame, but this invites the viewer to simply compare the mirrored halves of the image rather than interpret the image as a satisfying whole. Nearly is not good enough with this kind of image, and the alignment of the axis of symmetry and the equivalence of the two halves has to be perfect. Symmetry of line or of shape must be accompanied by perfect symmetry of pattern, colour or texture.

Reflections can be used to create a second half to an otherwise unsymmetrical scene. Photographers sometimes stretch the viewer's perceptual powers by taking a picture of only the reflection to force the eye to make out what real-world objects created that reflection.

Underpass (facing opposite, top)

Presented upright, this image of a reflection in a puddle in an underpass gets us guessing about the true nature of the real world it reflects.

Photographer: Wilson Tsoi.

Technical summary: Canon A80 digital compact at widest focal length of 11mm, equivalent to 35mm, 1/25 sec at f5.6, White Balance set for Cloudy, ISO 50, with minor saturation adjustment.

Beyond fashion (facing opposite, bottom)

The young model was shot out of hours in a play area, where a cheerful ambience has been created with music and food. The photographer uses a strongly symmetrical composition, contrasting colours and quirky posture to bring a sense of fun to this self-initiated project on shoes. The intense colour saturation comes from using ring flash, which delivers crisp, shadow-free lighting.

Photographer: Caroline Leeming.

Technical summary: Nikon D100, ring flash, 1/125sec at f8/11.

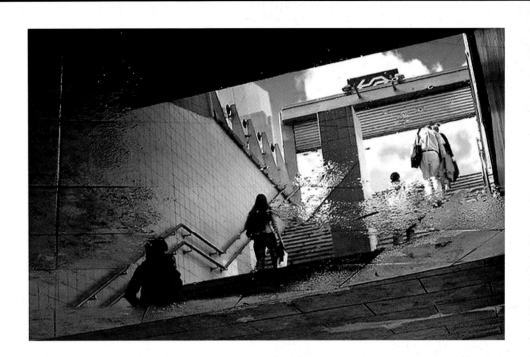

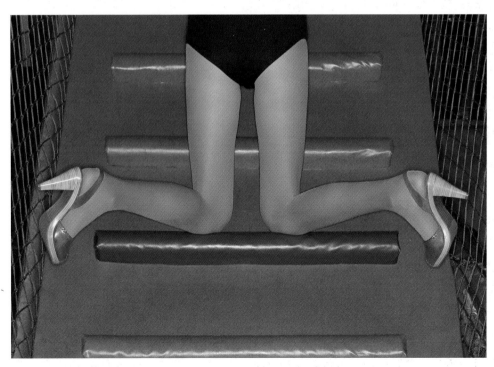

Symmetry and the face

The first task of a newborn baby is to learn to recognise its mother's face as soon as possible, as she is the source of food, love and security. From this point on we rapidly learn to recognise and compare visual patterns. Naturally, we become adept at picking out faces in crowds and comparing the slight asymmetries in a face that makes it unique. Plenty of research has been conducted to show that a symmetrical face with a good balance between the two halves is considered beautiful. Any asymmetry in the face is considered to have 'character', but any great imbalance in the features becomes a source of discomfort for the viewer. It is important to remember these deep-rooted psychological responses when taking portraits.

When a single lamp lights the face straight on, the lighting is flat and the form of the face and its textures are minimised. Side lighting is purposely used in portraiture to cast shadows to one side of the face (usually in a ratio of 4:1). This gently breaks up the symmetry of the face, modelling and emphasising its form from the shadows. Window light and a reflector used in this ratio can create the most flattering lighting for portraits. If the lighting ratio increases beyond 4:1, the contrast between the highlights and shadows increases, and even a perfectly symmetrical face will be cast adversely in unbalanced light. Similarly, our expectations of lighting from in front or from the side means that we find lighting from below the face strange or sinister.

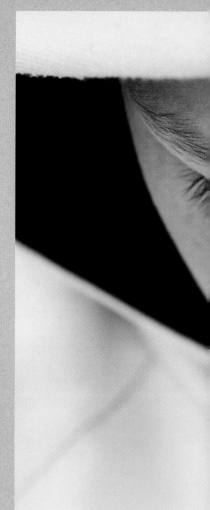

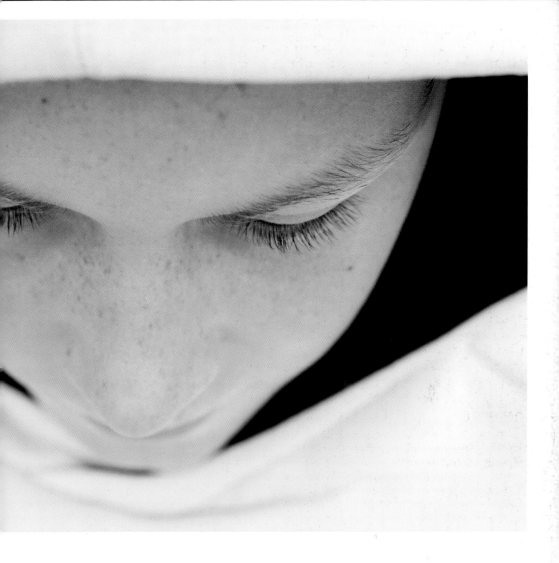

Martin (above)

A hooded top and unusually high viewpoint frame a face symmetrically. The colour of the clothing complements the skin tone, creating a dramatic V-shaped shadow. Neither the eyes nor the direction of gaze are visible, adding an element of intrigue.

Photographer: Nina Indset Andersen.

Technical summary: No camera details. Shot in shadow on a fairly sunny day with the contrast slightly enhanced in Photoshop.

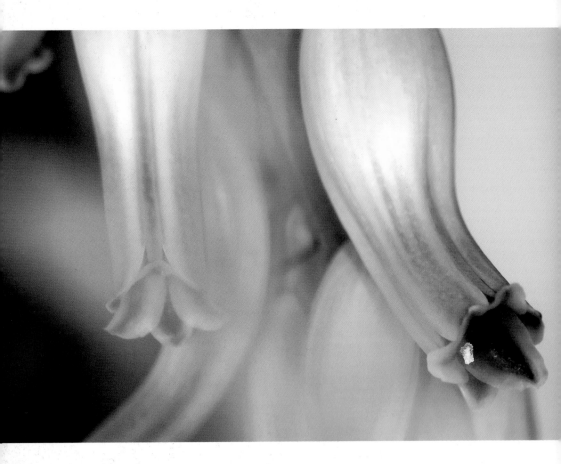

Agave flower (above)

The soft focus in this image emphasises shape, form and colour, and gracefully smudges foreground detail.

Photographer: David Präkel.

Technical summary: D100 70–300 Zoom Nikkor with Nikon +2.9 dioptre supplementary close-up attachment and SB-29 ring flash. Limited depth of field despite small aperture 1/180sec at f22, reduced further by focusing just in front of main flower.

Appearance of space

Nowadays, photography is called a 'lens-based medium', in recognition of the fact that sharp focus and lens blur are characteristics unique to the medium. An artist can create smudged effects working in paint and pencil but nothing that corresponds convincingly to progressive lens blur. In photography, it is generally assumed that sharpness indicates significance – although there are image makers who have purposefully subverted this convention by focusing beyond the subject.

Lenses with a long focal length have very shallow depths of field even when stopped down; very wide-angle lenses almost need no focusing, so great is their inherent depth of field. These differences can influence the choice of focal length – for example, use a long focal length lens where you want to have crisp focus, but a rapid fall off into blur.

The point of focus is important, especially with portraits where the eyes must be in perfect focus. It may be necessary to override the automatic focus on the camera to achieve precise or specific focusing effects. Switching to manual focus or using focus lock are two ways to achieve this.

The quality of the out-of-focus parts of the image can be important – especially in portraiture where a very soft, smooth quality may be required. The lens aperture is responsible for the quality of the blur and it will introduce its own shape into the out-of-focus highlights. The more circular the aperture, the more satisfying the blur. This was first noted by a camera enthusiast in Japan who used the term 'bokeh' to describe the quality of blur in a lens. Lenses which retain a circular rather than a flat-sided aperture as they stop down are highly rated for bokeh – the more blades in the lens iris (and therefore the more costly the lens), the better the bokeh. Cheap lenses produce six- or eight-sided out-of-focus highlights that can detract from the main subject.

1

2

3

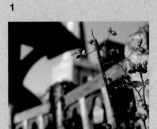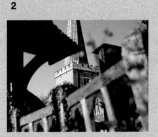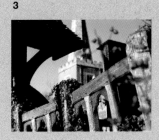

Selective focus: 1 Close focus; 2 Distant focus; 3 Mid-distance focus.

Depth of field

At maximum lens aperture – when the lens is fully open – focus is a very thin plane that drops through the subject, parallel to the plane of the film or the sensor in a digital camera. There is some depth of field, or acceptable sharpness, in front of and behind the true plane of focus, but this may not amount to much. As the lens aperture is reduced, or closed down, this apparent sharpness begins to extend further in front of and behind the plane where the lens is focused. The depth of field does not increase evenly in front and behind – as a rule of thumb it grows one-third in front of the

focus point and two-thirds behind. Any part of the subject falling within the 'depth of field' will appear acceptably sharp.

Use of the lens aperture gives photographers control over what appears sharp and what does not. Throwing the background out of focus behind the subject is a case for maximum aperture; getting the whole of a flower in focus is a case for carefully focusing some way across the flower head and stopping down the lens to achieve a depth of field that extends over the whole flower. Depth of field is reduced the closer the camera is to the subject, and the longer

f2.8 | Point of focus   f5.6

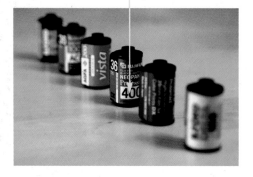 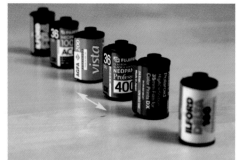

In these four photographs you can see how the depth of field increases as the lens aperture gets smaller.

the focal length of the lens used, the shallower the depth of field. A depth-of-field preview button (on SLR cameras) will show how much depth of field you will have at the taking aperture – focusing is always done at maximum aperture.

Hyperfocal focusing is a method of maximising depth of field and is often utilised by landscape photographers to get images that are sharp from foreground to background. An autofocus camera will focus on infinity (the furthest point) in these circumstances, which wastes a large part of the available depth of field. When a lens is

focused at infinity the near limit of its depth of field for the chosen aperture is called the hyperfocal distance. If your lens has one, this can be read off the lens depth-of-field scale. By shifting the focus to the hyperfocal distance the maximum depth of field can be achieved for that lens aperture. If the lens does not have a depth of field scale revert to the one-third/two-thirds advice.

f11

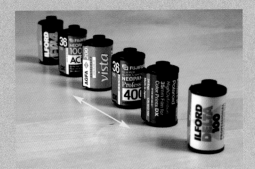

f22

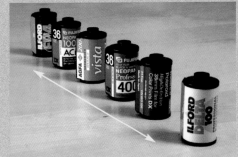

Foreground and background

Much landscape photography disappoints the photographer. The results can seem too flat, as if they are bound by the two dimensions of the medium. Images can entice the viewer into the small, framed world. One way of achieving that is to emphasise the illusion of depth in the image. Simply lowering the viewpoint will connect the viewer to the landscape in a dramatic way. An image taken from a lower viewpoint will emphasise the foreground, increasing the apparent depth in the image. Landscapes taken from a conventional standing viewpoint are more detached from the viewer. Wide-angle lenses favour foreground objects, enable closer working and have inherently greater depth of field.

In art, any shape that overlaps and hides the background or another shape is a foreground object. Without overlap the two shapes might be misinterpreted as side by side on a flat plane. Careful choice of viewpoint can overlap a foreground frame or part of a larger foreground object to increase the sense of depth. This holds good for any form of photography and not just landscapes. Shadows also provide clues about depth as they recede along the perspective planes of the image.

Limiting the depth of field will throw the foreground or background selectively out of focus. This shifts the emphasis within the image. Some photographers will intentionally focus beyond the subject in the foreground to create an element of ambiguity or doubt, as the apparent subject will then appear out of focus in front of a sharply focused world.

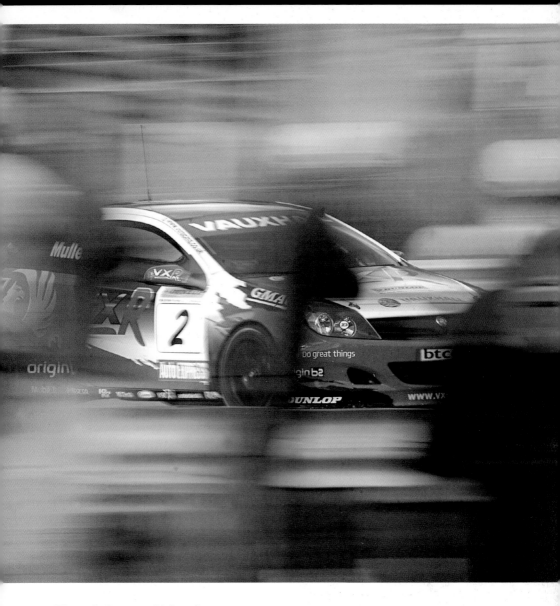

Through the crowd (above)

The subject is in the background, but despite this the viewer 'feels' as though he or she is in there with the driver, former touring car champion Yvan Muller, at the British Touring Car event, Brands Hatch. The camera was manually pre-focused and panned with a slow-enough shutter speed to blur the foreground crowd despite the depth of field available at that working aperture.

Photographer: David Elsworth.

Technical summary: Nikon D100 with 70–300mm Sigma zoom, 1/30th sec at f22, ISO 200.

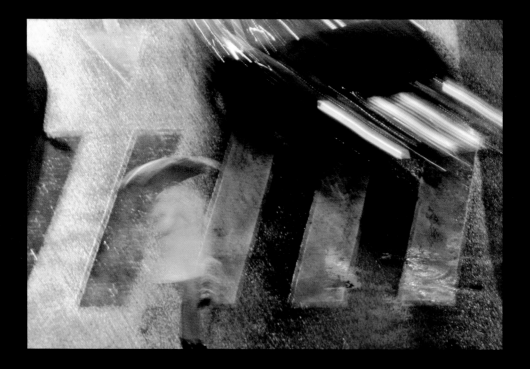

Selecting lens aperture and the point of focus gives the photographer control over which part and how much of the image is sharp. In contrast, shutter speed gives photographers control over the appearance of motion in the image. The choice for the photographer is either to freeze motion or to emphasise and blur it.

This chapter considers very different approaches to how passing time is shown in images. Slow shutter speeds and longer time exposures can portray the movement of objects through the frame, creating mesmerising blurring shapes that track the movement of the subject. Other impressive effects include capturing the subject completely still while others move around it over a long exposure, creating a fascinating differential between stillness and movement.

Fast shutter speeds and high-speed electronic flash have produced unique images that show time standing still, enabling us to analyse phenomena previously unrecorded, such as the passage of a bullet through a piece of fruit or the bursting of a balloon. Modern cameras can combine time exposure and flash to create images where the subject is frozen in a blurry, moving world. There is never-ending appeal in the way the camera seems to stop the clock.

In any photographic situation, there is an ideal or optimum moment to capture the image when the dynamic world and the static elements gel perfectly. Photographer Henri Cartier-Bresson coined the term 'decisive moment' to describe this phenomenon. We'll look at capturing the 'decisive moment' in more detail, and also cover how sequential, rather than single, images can show the passing of time in revealing ways.

Zebra crossing (facing opposite)
The car and pedestrian are both moving through the rain, but their different speeds create diverse effects. The colours, graphic road markings, moving lights and solitary figure create a memorable image that has the quality of a captured glance – a unique conjunction.

Photographer: Felipe Rodriguez.

Technical summary: Fujifilm FInepix S2 Pro, Nikkor 80–400mm VR, 0.3 sec at f5.3, ISO 1600, contrast increased in Photoshop.

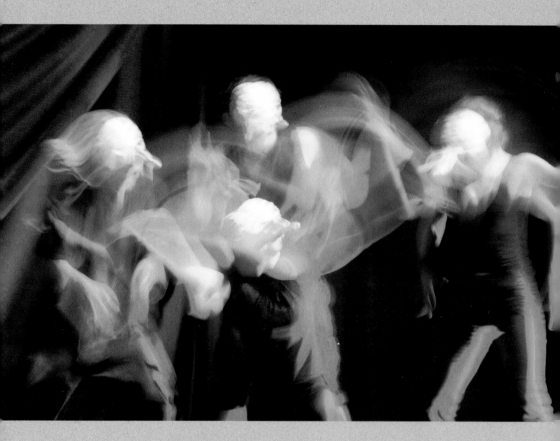

Masks (above)

Taken during a dress rehearsal of Shakespeare's *The Tempest*. 'Miranda's Dream' was lit
only by the roving spotlights so the performers moved in and through pools of moving light.
A slow-sync flash exposure with flash illumination was made during a long exposure to capture
movement and ambience.

Photographer: Sam Henderson.

Technical summary: Nikon D100 with Tamron 24–135mm lens, ISO 800 to achieve acceptable depth of field and
1/15 sec exposure, off-camera Nikon Speedlight flash, fired manually.

Time passing

In 1826, Joseph Nicéphore Niépce placed a photosensitive metal plate into a 'camera obscura' (a lens and box with a viewing screen, used to assist artists with composition) and pointed it out of his garret workroom window. After an eight-hour exposure, he 'developed' the image with a mixture of lavender oil and petroleum to reveal a view of the courtyard and its buildings with trees and landscape beyond. While this was the first ever permanent 'photograph' from nature, Niépce was apparently dissatisfied by the unnatural quality of the light and shadows. During the day-long exposure the sun had moved across the sky, unnaturally illuminating both sides of the courtyard.

Long exposures will show any movement of the subject during the period that the camera shutter is open. In this way, photographers can depict movement in an otherwise static medium. There is an advantage and disadvantage to blurred movement. The downside is that detail is lost, but in its favour, colour becomes more enhanced and the line of motion through the image is revealed. Popular effects include blurred tail- and headlights on moving vehicles and the blurred rush of water over rocks or from a waterfall. These images have become photographic clichés, but original and creative examples can still be revealing.

With modern, high-sensitivity photographic materials, time exposures need to be made in low-light conditions or with the use of neutral density filters. This is to achieve the long exposure times that will show movement of light and subject during exposure. The effects can vary immensely. For example, a stationary camera can show the movement of a subject against a still background during a long exposure. Camera movement during a time exposure can create an overall blur. Exposure times for such effects are – even among professionals – largely a case of trial and error or bracketing (a series of correct, under- and overexposed images) to produce the desired effect. With film, very long exposures cause a breakdown in the linear relationship between exposure time and the amount of light, which can cause unwanted shifts in colour. With digital cameras, long exposures can produce unwanted noise, and many models feature a special long-exposure noise reduction capture setting to moderate this.

Moments

In the early days of photography, exposures took tens of seconds rather than fractions of a second. But as photographic materials improved to become more sensitive to light, it was possible to reduce exposure times dramatically. This improvement in materials made it possible to slice time into perfectly still moments, forever poised and motionless. Most modern cameras feature shutter speeds of 1/1000 sec or faster and, with appropriate film speeds or ISO sensitivity setting for digital, can freeze the moment. High-energy studio flashes can create a light duration of about 1/10,000sec to capture something as transitory as a water splash, frozen in time.

Photographic images such as these are endlessly fascinating and bear repeated viewing as they show us something we cannot see with the unaided eye, and also play with our sense of expectation. We know what should happen next, but in the image it never does.

Sports photographers learn to develop the skill of anticipation to capture perfectly frozen moments of play. They focus on a seemingly irrelevant section of grass on a pitch where they wait for the action to occur. Sometimes autofocus – even of the predictive variety – is not fast enough, and they have to rely on manual pre-focusing. Having enough light to be able to stop the lens down to get the subject somewhere in the depth of field bracket is a bonus. Camera panning is sometimes necessary to catch a fast-moving subject. This means moving the camera with the subject, keeping it sharp against a motion-blurred background.

Happy Sunday morning (facing opposite)

She is suspended forever in mid-air with legs akimbo. The photographer required total concentration to retain the background composition while anticipating where the little girl would bounce next. The subject momentarily stops at the peak of the bounce, which enables the photographer to use a slightly slower shutter speed than would be otherwise required. Strong natural light was balanced with flash.

Photographer: Nina Indset Andersen.

Technical summary: No camera details. Contrast adjusted in Photoshop.

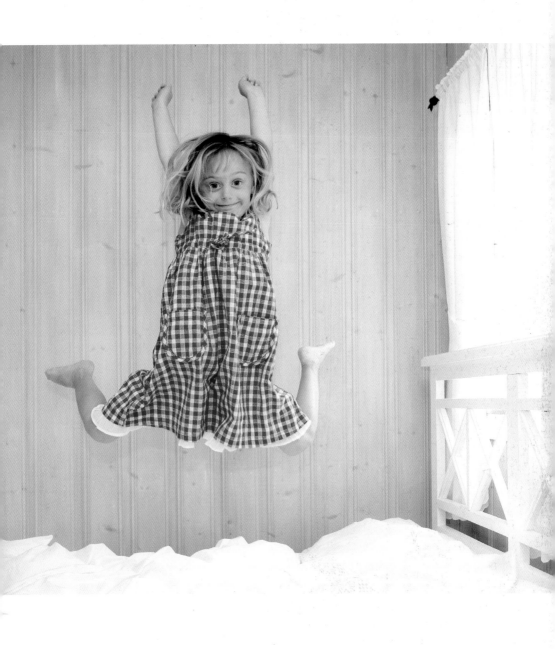

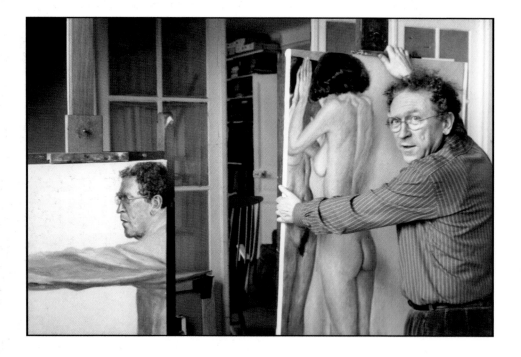

The decisive moment

Cartier-Bresson's 'decisive moment' is a much misunderstood concept. The phrase was, in fact, coined by his American publisher, an improvement of the literal translation 'Images on the run' for his 1952 portfolio. The 'decisive moment' means that in each picture-taking situation, there is only one moment when all the compositional and emotional elements in the picture coincide at their most powerful – as a photographer, you had better be able to recognise it!

Cartier-Bresson did not simply snap one critical picture, however, but would make a series of images. In a film showing him at work, he can be seen taking pictures almost continuously, without even having his camera – invariably a Leica rangefinder – close to his eye. His talent was to recognise the moment of the coming together of the emotional and compositional elements and to find that frame among his images.

To see such arrangements, to trigger the shutter to catch them and to be able to repeat this quality of observation is what makes his body of photographic work so remarkable.

The decisive moment is not simply capturing the peak of the action, as a sports photographer might do. Studying Cartier-Bresson's portraits of artists shows the principle at work. In an extraordinary portrait of the artist Alberto Giacometti (1961), Cartier-Bresson captures the artist as he unintentionally, but precisely, mirrors his own statues; the long shutter speed emphasises his movement and separates Giacometti from his work in just one dimension. Similarly, in Cartier-Bresson's portrait of Avigdor Arikha, there is no set up, no posing. It took an instant to capture the moment in which the artist moves a canvas and fleetingly mirrors his self-portrait at the left of the frame.

Portrait of the artist Avigdor Arikha (facing opposite)

Compositionally, it might be argued that this is a poorly created image, with the doorframe and dark band dividing the image down the middle. The right-hand side of the image would stand alone as a superb portrait of the artist; to have included the self-portrait on the left is simply remarkable. The pose of the nude in the painting enhances this uncanny moment, as does the artist's careful, almost reverential, grip on her canvas. Only in this instant has everything come together.

Photographer: Henri Cartier-Bresson.

Technical summary: None provided.

Sequences

Control of shutter speed enables photographers to represent time frozen or blurred in a single image. However, some photographers go further in their quest to overcome the limitations of depicting passing time in just one image.

In 1877, photographer Eadweard Muybridge used a sequence of photographs to help settle a bet. In a series of rapidly taken images, he demonstrated that a galloping horse can have all four feet off the ground at one time. Muybridge used a series of cameras, triggered by the horse running through shutter strings stretched across its path, to produce an elegant sequence of images. Though he was attempting to freeze action, he had unwittingly laid the basis for creating 'moving pictures'. What fascinated contemporary viewers was the way in which complex actions were broken down into individual images. Sequences provide the viewer with a way to fast-forward and rewind time by jumping ahead or looking back through a sequence. They show the progress of an event or create a narrative.

Muybridge helped lay the foundations for the movie industry. Although he did not know it at the time, the storyboard format – which shows the unfolding of a story through a sequence of images over a period of time – is now familiar from movie and video planning. Photographers use the storyboard as a source of inspiration – thus, in creative terms, the idea of 'sequence' has come full circle.

In striking contrast to the sequence, it is possible to create multiple exposures in a single image by using a powerful strobe flash that pulses light during a single exposure. With multiple exposures the images are overlaid one on top of the other rather than in sequential order.

Bogeyman (facing opposite)

This sequence of images explores fear in a similar way to a movie storyboard, but packs in more detail. A child's nightmare comes alive as the spooky coat and hat become a real bogeyman when the young girl falls asleep. The narrative is clear, but the viewer is uncertain as to whether it is real or imagined.

Photographer: Duane Michals.

Technical summary: None provided.

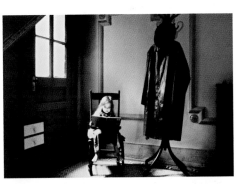
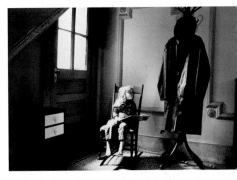
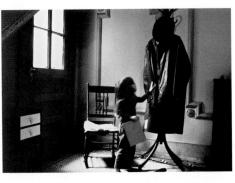
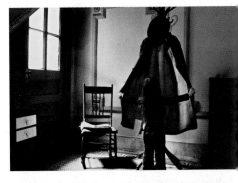
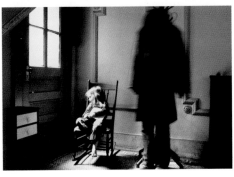
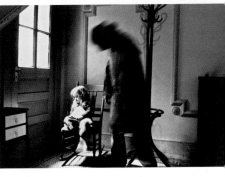

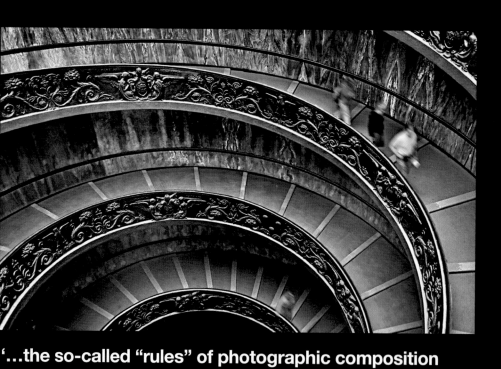

'…the so-called "rules" of photographic composition are… invalid, irrelevant and immaterial… There are no rules of composition in photography, only good photographs.' Ansel Adams (landscape photographer)

Armed with knowledge about geometry and proportion, how do photographers tackle composition in the real world? In some situations, such as conventional landscape photography, the photographer has control of certain aspects only: they must wait for the right light, are at the mercy of the weather and their choice of viewpoint is critical. In complete contrast, the still-life photographer is able to control every detail, from subject arrangement to lighting. Still-life photographers often impose limits on their work by studying still-life paintings or by exploring traditions of the medium – for example, photographing a single, perfect flower. Fine-art photography shares some similarities with still life, irrespective of its subject matter, as the artist-photographer often researches and revives alternative or early photographic techniques, sometimes in combination with modern techniques.

Portraiture is an enduring subject for photography. Many portraitists are motivated by the endless variations of the human face. Moving out of the studio into the sitter's own environment opens up the possibilities, revealing more about a subject's personality and interests. As with portraiture, figure work – depicting the nude human form – is equally enduring; the human body is a classic subject for experimenting with shape, light and texture.

Composition is a much more difficult prospect for the documentary or action photographer, but is, if anything more important in translating the narrative of a moment to the viewer. The greatest images from both genres have come about when technical excellence has been combined with vigorous composition.

In the commercial world, composition may be the skilful interpretation of another person's visual ideas. In advertising and editorial photography, the dictates of the art director or picture editor are key to what kind of image the photographer takes. An image may have to be composed around a prescribed design.

This chapter considers how to use the ideas described above in many practical situations to demonstrate how central composition is to the process.

Vatican stairs (facing opposite)
Careful geometric composition is applied to a traveller's photograph of tourists climbing a great spiral staircase in the Vatican, Rome. Photographic technique is used to blur the moving people, contrasting them with the precision and solidity of the architecture. This also turns the tourists into splashes of colour in the overall achromatic view, adding a degree of drama and showing the photographer's keen awareness of colour.

Photographer: Trine Sirnes Thorne.

Technical summary: Canon EOS 300D (Digital Rebel) with Canon ER-S 18–55mm lens, ISO 100, the image was selectively desaturated and the background toned, keeping colour in the subjects on the stairs.

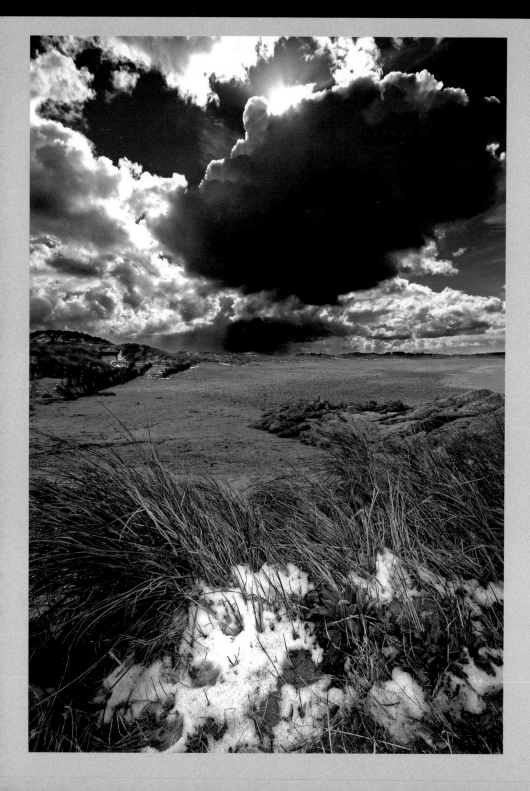

Landscape

Landscape photography incorporates all the elements of composition, but writ large, hence its popularity. With landscape composition, the photographer waits for light to reveal texture, such as geological and archaeological features, to advantage. Shape and form are revealed by the illumination of the constantly moving sun and moon over the forms of the land. The changing seasons clothe the land in wide-ranging colours.

Landscape composition is not simply the arrangement of elements in the camera frame, but an appreciation that the image can be transformed by changes in lighting over which the photographer has no control. While the photographer has control over the selection of viewpoint, he or she is subject to the will of nature when it comes to lighting and can only wait and observe. The height and direction of the sun determine light in the landscape and that is dictated by the time of day and the season. Some landscapes –

such as north-facing coastlines in the northern hemisphere – are never lit by direct sun. Patience is the greatest virtue. 'Sun finder' charts offer guidance on the placement of the sun and sun compasses can help establish how the light will fall across a given landscape. Of course careful research in books and magazines helps, too. While these aids provide helpful preparation for a trip, experience is the only real solution. Certain famous locations have very limited times in the year when they can be photographed – when light penetrates a gorge to illuminate a particular feature, for example.

With landscape photography, before the photographer composes the images, he or she must consider a sense of place. This awareness is what motivates the landscape photographer to express emotional responses to the landscape through photographic means. Without this honesty, landscape photographs will lack emotional depth.

Land and sky (right)

The ultra wide-angle lens, with its massive depth of field, enhances the foreground and emphasises the sky, creating deep perspective and enticing the viewer into the image. The patch of snow balances the cloud formation.

Photographer: Marina Cano.

Technical summary: Canon 20D with Canon 10–22mm EF-S, 1/125 sec at f11, ISO 200.

Still life

Still life is defined as an arrangement of inanimate (lifeless) objects. It has been a popular discipline with painters and photographers – perhaps, in part, because of its adaptability. In this way, still-life composition is in complete contrast to landscape photography. With a still life everything is under the photographer's control, from the choice of subject to the background and the quality of light. For this reason alone, it requires more discipline, as there are many more variables to play with. It is worth studying the great still-life painters. Look principally at the compositional balance created in their arrangements and how they handle light.

Many photographers approach their still life subjects as simple, geometric solids (cubes, cones, spheres). Some have practised with little more than a set of wooden or paper forms and a single light source. In fact, almost any object will do for still life, as it is shape and form that is of principal interest.

For quality, it is best to work with a large-format camera. It is easier to use a 5 x 4 transparency mask as a frame to establish the viewpoint than to drag the camera around. To do this, hold the frame in front of one eye at roughly the same distance as the focal length of the lens you intend to use.

The simplest lighting is from a single light source, accompanied by a reflector to control the lighting ratio across the set. The background can be lit independently. Though the greatest still-life control comes from having mastery of the studio lights, still life outdoors can be even more rewarding, using only the natural light and perhaps a corner of a garden as a setting for pre-selected props. Artist-photographers such as Andy Goldsworthy and Chris Drury create and record organic still lifes from materials found in the environment. Their approach and choice of location is diverse and can include found still lifes in such locations as street markets and the corners of potting sheds.

Elevation (facing opposite)

Selective focus and careful use of depth of field turn this simplest of still-life images, comprising little more than a glass marble and roll of plastic, into a contemplation of colour and form. The roll and marble being of the same diameter and lying on the same axis give the image 'incident', the sense that the marble has appeared from the folds behind it and stopped.

Photographer: Trine Sirnes Thorne.

Technical summary: Nikon Coolpix 880.

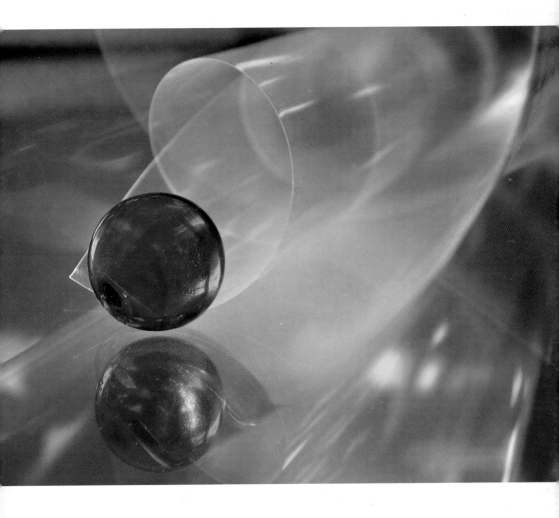

Portrait

The human face is endlessly fascinating. It is a given form with infinite variations. Portraits can be handled in either a formal or a candid style. In a formal portrait, the sitter and photographer have a consensual understanding of the event and usually work together to create the image. Candid portraits are taken when the subject is unaware of the photographer and is more relaxed and natural. Both kinds of portraits are revealing in different ways.

Though studio work is often more closely associated with formal portraits, good candid pictures can also be taken in the studio. Formal portraits can be taken on location away from the studio. Simple window light and a reflector can be all that is needed for a formal portrait of a sitter relaxed in their own surroundings.

To find the 'essence' of a personality it is often most effective to focus solely on the face. Environmental portraiture in contrast includes the subject's surroundings to provide contrast and context, such as their occupation or passion, or to reflect their status.

Photographing two or more people formally or informally can be a challenge. How the sitters use their personal space and respond to each other affects how the viewer interprets the image. Individuals positioned too closely together may appear to be tense and uncomfortable, despite their 'fake' smiles. With subjects who are known to each other, the photographer can explore the dynamics of their relationship.

Sisters (facing opposite)

The tightest of in-camera crops captures a moment of intimacy between two sisters, made all the stronger by showing only one half of each face – there is a whole face in this picture, but it belongs to two people! Cutting out the background and details of clothes and hairstyles creates a timeless quality.

Photographer: Nina Indset Andersen.

Technical summary: No camera details. Taken in shadow on a very bright, sunny day with a white reflector to add modelling to the faces, contrast adjusted in Photoshop and converted to black and white.

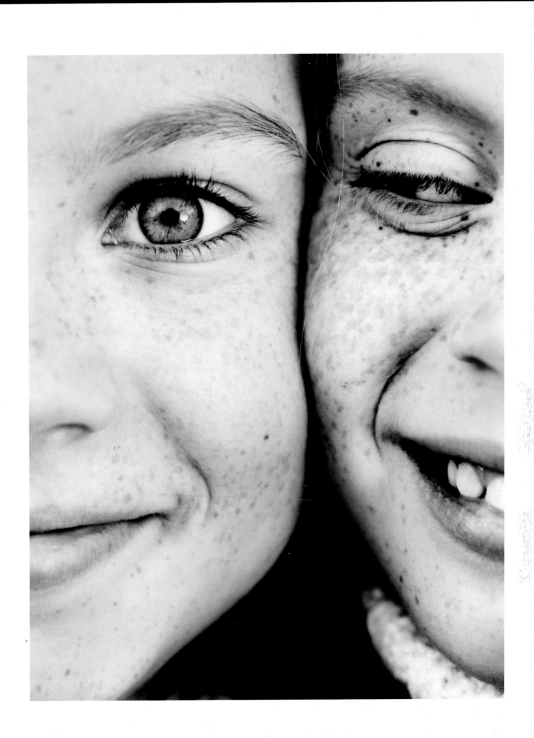

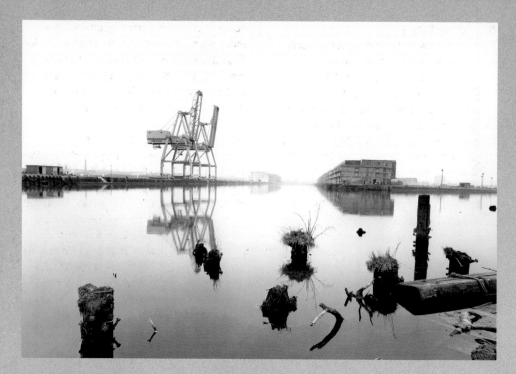

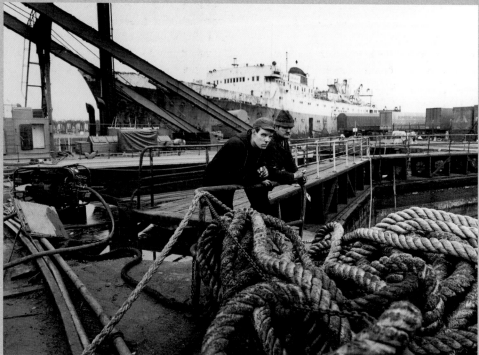

Documentary

Because its subject matter is not primarily aesthetic, the role of composition in documentary photography can be underestimated. Yet it is only well-composed images that will catch the public attention. Documentary photography is closely linked to photojournalism and reportage, but may not share their sense of 'newsworthiness'. By definition, it is a form of photography that creates a document, a record. Even its practitioners disagree about its objectivity or, as some would argue, lack of it. The contradiction at the heart of documentary photography is that the most meaningful images can only be made through close engagement with, and understanding of, the subject. However, that level of involvement can challenge a wholly objective position. Whatever your feelings about that, it can be one of the most rewarding forms of image-making.

Documentary photography is typically project-based, in as much as a photographer will take either a commission or a subject of their choice and create a series of images, usually over a period of time, to document the subject. Despite requiring objectivity, some documentary photographers have a more overtly political agenda and they make this quite clear, while there are those who want to create change by applying pressure via their images – this is province of the so-called 'concerned photographer'.

The images shown opposite are by photographer John Darwell, published in the 1986 book *The Big Ditch* (now out of print). Though Darwell disavows documentary photography, largely on the grounds outlined above, he concurs with the description of himself as an 'independent' photographer. His study of the Manchester Ship Canal was originally made in the 1980s and still tours in exhibition today. Darwell describes the project: 'My intention was to capture every aspect of the canal at a time when its future lay in the balance, from the boat crews and swing bridge keepers to the industry on its banks to the landscape through which it passes, and in many cases formed, this work stands as a testament to a bygone age.' Subsequent projects have included industrial change, foot and mouth disease, the representation of mental health and the history of nuclear technology.

No. 9 dock (facing opposite, top) and Ship dismantlers (bottom)

These images are taken from *The Big Ditch*, a study of the Manchester Ship Canal in the 1980s.

Photographer: John Darwell.

Technical summary: 6 x 9cm format FP4 film with a 50mm wide-angle lens, prints (in a limited edition of ten) made on Agfa Record Rapid 24 x 20in paper and selenium-toned.

Figure

We are endlessly fascinated by our own representation – whether faces in portraits, the clothed body, in fashion photography, for example, or with the unique variations of the nude form. The nude has a long and controversial, but compelling history, from the human body as classical study of form and light, via glamour photography, to pornography. The approach to and motivation for each of these genres may be radically different – from fine art to commercial to exploitative, but any photography of the human body is likely to provoke an emotional response and some kind of debate. The boundaries shift over time with public taste and the law. It is worth considering where the boundaries are for you and your own audience.

There is a difference between a picture of a naked person and a nude. To be naked is to be vulnerable, intimate, whereas the nude is depersonalised. Techniques for photographing the nude often include framing the torso to crop out the face.

Facial expressions, like props, can introduce loaded messages into your images. If you do decide to include a person's face consider that a made-up face and a naked body together may carry an undesirable message. As well as an aesthetic approach, nude photography requires plenty of practical organisation: for location, warmth and privacy, and ensuring that there are no marks on the body from underclothes. Consider too whether your sitter – male or female – wishes to be chaperoned.

Compositionally, it is difficult not to be overwhelmed. In the studio, it is best to start with uncomplicated lighting and some simple poses – talk through poses with your model before you begin photography, perhaps referencing classic nude images to clarify what you are looking for. Use lighting to reveal the body's form and textures, exploring the abstraction of shape and line or emphasising sensuality. Shooting the nude in the landscape requires exceptional skill and careful consideration of matters of taste.

Nude (facing opposite)

This is a timeless, classic nude study that uses low-key presentation and a simply framed torso. The left-to-right diagonal rises across the picture giving a sense of height and stature. The lighting is controlled to perfection, revealing form and texture on the upper body and leading leg and silhouetting the body shape against the backdrop. The weight of the body is also hinted at by the folds of cloth on the surface on which the model sits where she supports herself on her unseen, outstretched arm.

Photographer: Eric Kellerman.

Technical summary: Nikon D70 with Nikon 28–70mm zoom lens, 1/125 sec at f5.6, ISO 200, cropped and converted to black and white in Photoshop.

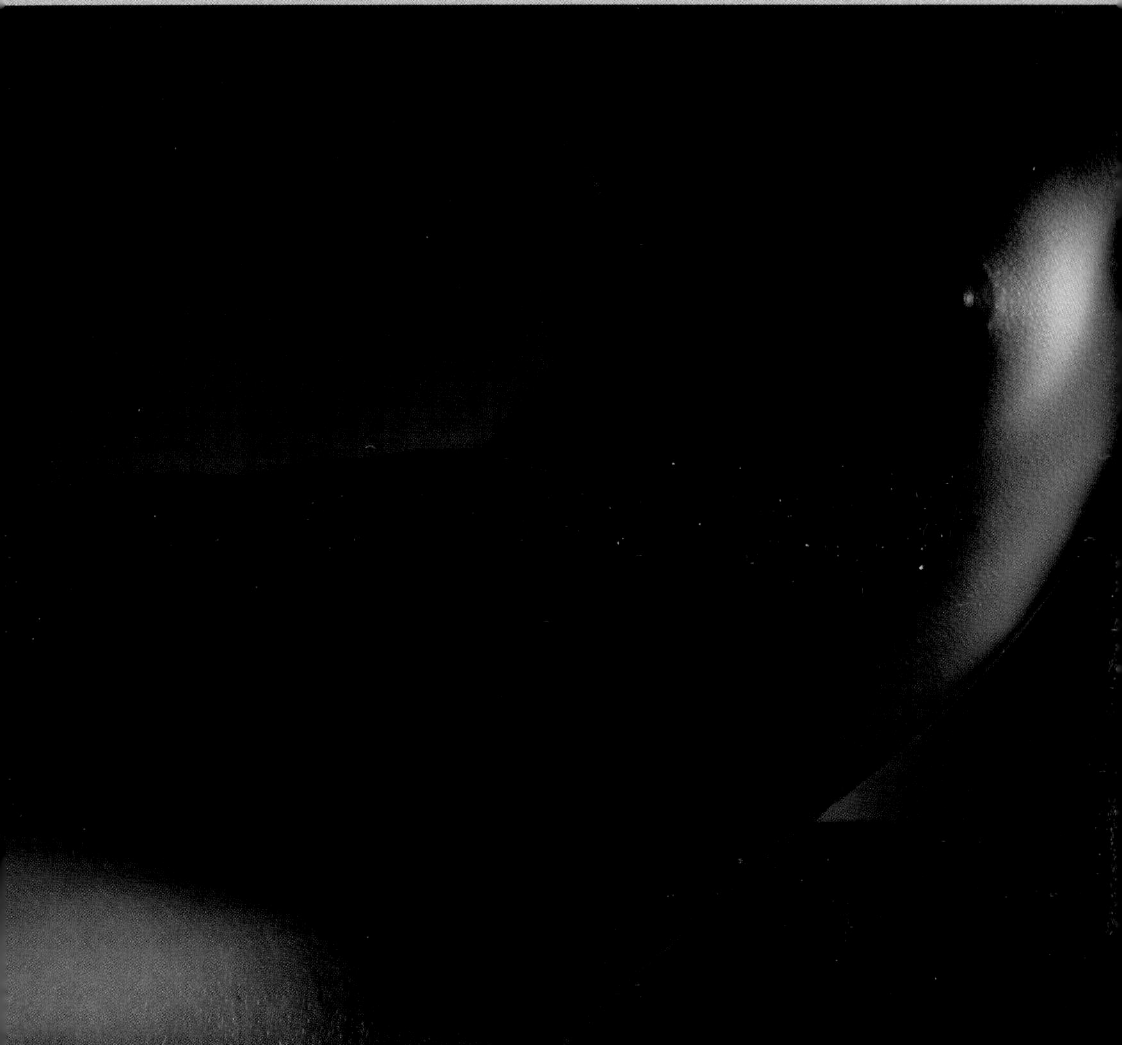

Figure 144_145

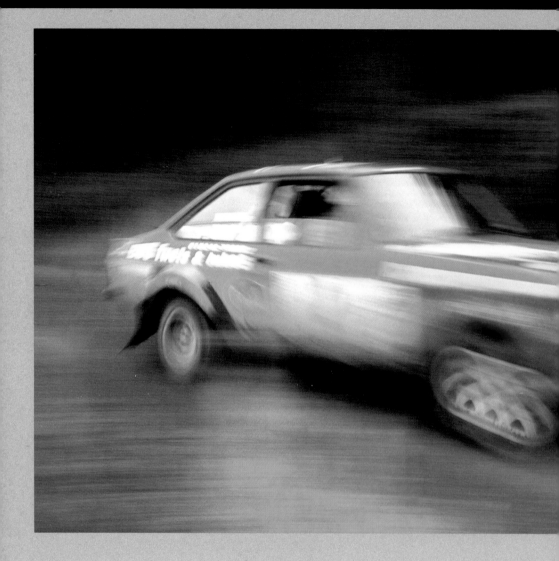

MKII Escort (above)

After his degree, David Elsworth specialised in motorsport photography. This image was taken on the Grizedale Forest Rally in December 2002. Elsworth explains: 'The Escort was travelling down a straight at around 70mph. The shot was at 1/30sec while panning and pulling the lens out from full zoom at 35mm to 19mm.' Elsworth's dramatic, close-up image pitches the viewer into the action. With this image, Elsworth transcends the standard sports image by translating the excitement of the moment.

Photographer: David Elsworth.

Technical summary: Canon EOS 5 with 19–35mm lens, Fuji Sensia 400 film.

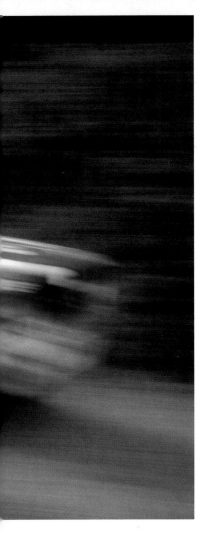

Action/sports

Outstanding sporting images transcend interest in the game or sport. They say something about human endeavour or achievement. It is not enough to simply capture the peak of the action. While this may appeal to the sports fan, there has to be an additional element to capture the interest of the general viewer. Strong composition can give action shots this backbone.

To some extent, with sport, the subject matter may be much more familiar to the photographer. He or she may already be familiar with the rules of the game, but what is impressive – and essential to the job – is their ability to pre-visualise and react to rapidly changing events. For the sports photographer, composition must be unconscious and immediate. Simply capturing the event can be difficult enough – as one ex-*New York Times* sports photographer put it: 'If you see it happen in the viewfinder you haven't caught it on film.' Anticipation is everything. Sports photographers need situational awareness and a sixth sense to anticipate the exceptional event before it happens.

Photographers must also be aware of what is going on beyond the field of play. Quite often, collateral events make the great images from sporting moments. These may be happening in the crowd rather than on the field. The great reaction shots are often scooped just before and after play. These images provide the human element, defining the doubts, despair, triumphs and thrills of the moment. Images such as these are the outcome of the photographer's well-honed sense of opportunism.

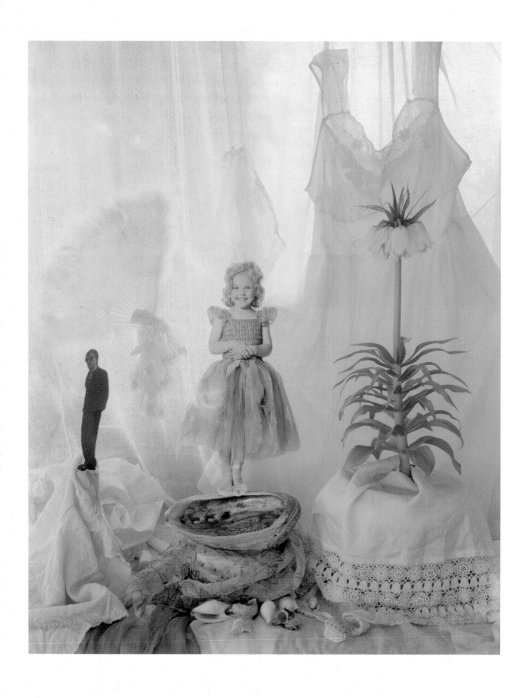

Fine art

Some photographic genres merge or crossover with others and it is often the context of the image that defines it. Fine-art photography is a case in point. It is possibly one of the most misunderstood of the photographic genres. For our purposes, fine-art photography is that which is undertaken for its aesthetic values alone.

The artist-photographer uses the photographic medium as a vehicle for creative self-expression and their work is often highly constructed to produce particular meanings. This might involve complex manipulations of materials, props, backgrounds and locations or incorporate alternative or historic processes, possibly in combination with modern digital techniques.

Artist-photographer Karen Melvin is interested in portraiture and self-portraiture. She has worked on a series of still-life photographs on this theme, collectively entitled 'Paper Dolls'. The series explores time, memory and family relationships, connecting the private world of everyday events with the mythology of fairy tales. The 'paper dolls' are black- and-white photographic figures produced by the artist for use in her colour images.

Working collaboratively with friends and family, Melvin creates improvised situations involving play with costumes and masks to create these figures. The photographic cut-out paper dolls are placed in relationship with other objects in the studio or locations in created 'playgrounds' full of personal associations and connections, inspired by folk tales and myths.

In compositional terms, the images are quite unusual and offer specific challenges for the photographer. They mix two- and three-dimensional objects, which requires careful lighting and sensitivity to scale and proportion. Using the photorealistic miniatures and everyday objects enables Melvin to explore the social dynamics in the relationships between family members, old and young, male and female or parent and child. Melvin accesses the fantasy world of her childhood play and reflects on the innocence and fragility of her grandchildren. The still-life arrangements are then re-photographed on large-format colour negative film, the colour rebalanced in Adobe Photoshop and printed as large fine-art prints to exploit the full range of detail. Her work demonstrates the complex relationship between motive and execution required for fine-art photography.

Family (facing opposite)

This image was one of the first in a series of 25 'Paper Doll' images.

Photographer: Karen Melvin.

Technical summary: MPP 5 x 4 view camera, mixed daylight and flash, Fuji NPS colour negative scanned on Nikon LS4500AF scanner, 30 x 40in colour exhibition prints from Epson 7600 wide-format printer on Hahnemuhle Cotton Rag 300g paper.

Advertising

Composition plays quite a different role in advertising photography. Composing images for use in adverts requires the photographer to consider how the image may be used beyond its taking. Will text be overlaid on the image? Will the image work alongside other images? Will it be used for magazine publishing or on the Web? Photographers tend to use large-format view cameras for this kind of work, as they offer complete control of perspective and depth of field – regardless of whether they are equipped with a film or digital back – and because the image size is already large, they produce the highest-quality images. Elements such as headlines or copy must be incorporated into the overall look of the image. Even in the digital era, tracing paper and wax crayons are still used to plan complex images where space needs to be created for text overlaying an image or for a secondary image or illustration. The large ground-glass screens on large-format canvas make this easy.

As incomplete material, advertising images can look quite unbalanced, with lots of space around the frame, waiting to be overlaid with text or other images. The photographer must consider using an appropriate density of tone or contrasting colour so that text can stand out clearly against the image, especially if the image is to be used behind text. The art director usually dictates the required look and the photographer must respect this choice when shooting and lighting in the studio. Placing text onto an image can have a dramatic effect on the perception of depth and needs to be taken into account early on in the process.

Anti-smoking health and beauty (facing opposite, top)

A strong visual health message delivered through contrasts. The perfect symmetry of the jar and the dynamic angle of the cigarette butt; the soft, light tones and the dark, sharp image of the ash add to the tension created by the violent stubbing out of a cigarette in a pot of face cream. It all shouts: 'Smoking will damage your looks.' The incredible detail of a large-format image makes the message even more intense.

Photographer: Kevin Summers Photography.

Art direction: Damian Collins.

Technical summary: 10 x 8 film camera with 240mm lens, Fuji Velvia 50 RVP.

Crystal Cruises Iron (facing opposite, bottom)

A clever and direct visual metaphor where the smoothing iron serenely steams through a sea of blue fabric. The crop adds immediacy and tension.

Photographer: Kevin Summers Photography.

Technical summary: 10 x 8 film camera with 240mm lens, Fuji Velvia 50 RVP.

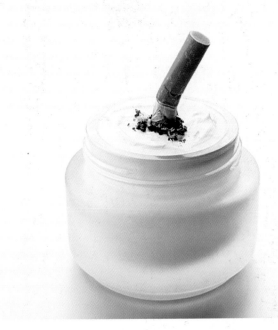

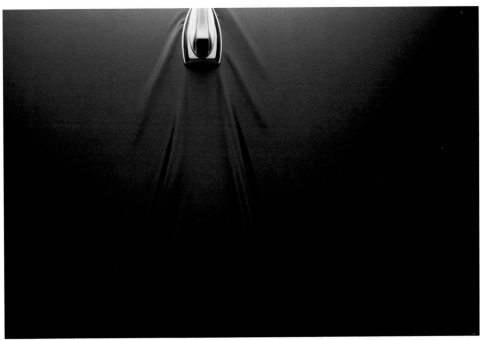

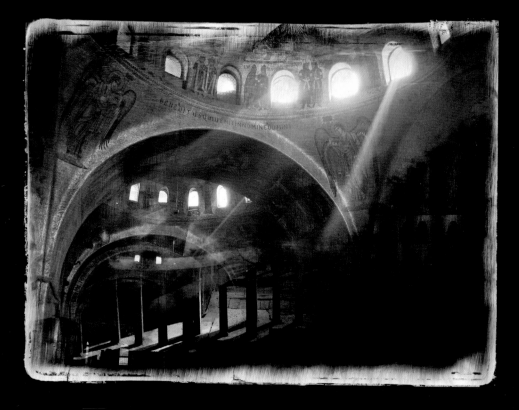

'Trust that little voice in your head that says
"Wouldn't it be interesting if..." and then do it.'
Duane Michals (photographer)

In this final section of the book, we bring together the ideas from previous chapters and consider how to develop a personal style, to discover ways to create inventive and thought-provoking images. We'll look at the importance of knowing in advance what kind of image is required from a photographic situation, and finding solutions to photographic problems before you even pick up a camera.

The 'Explore, isolate, organise' section looks at the mechanism of composition as theorised by photographer Andreas Feininger, which promotes pre-visualisation, 'working' the subject to develop new photographic solutions and using simple compositional rules to give order and coherence to an image.

Knowing the rules is one thing, but what happens when the photographer breaks or bends the 'rules' of composition? We look at techniques for deliberately incorporating imbalance in images by going against the conventions, and methods for creative cropping to create an effect. We explore the use of humour in the image, analysing why we find certain pictures amusing and how you can be best prepared to take advantage of comic photo opportunities. Contrast is another effective compositional tool. We look at the power of contrasting moods and creating contrast between subjects to add tension and dynamism to an image. Colour is an immense subject in its own right, but we'll take a brief look at how colour works with composition to create abstract effects.

Digital technology has already pushed so many boundaries in photography and created new opportunities for image-making. There are advantages and disadvantages to working digitally and using image-editing software and we'll look at this in more detail.

We'll conclude by exploring ways to incorporate approaches to composition in your own image-making.

Venezia (facing opposite)
Personal vision needs only inspiration. This is a digital composite image of Venice. Two images were layered with the frame and sepia-style toning applied digitally. The light rays are authentic.
Photographer: Jean Sébastien Monzani.
Technical summary: 3.2MPx Canon Powershot S30, 1/30sec at f2.8, ISO 200.

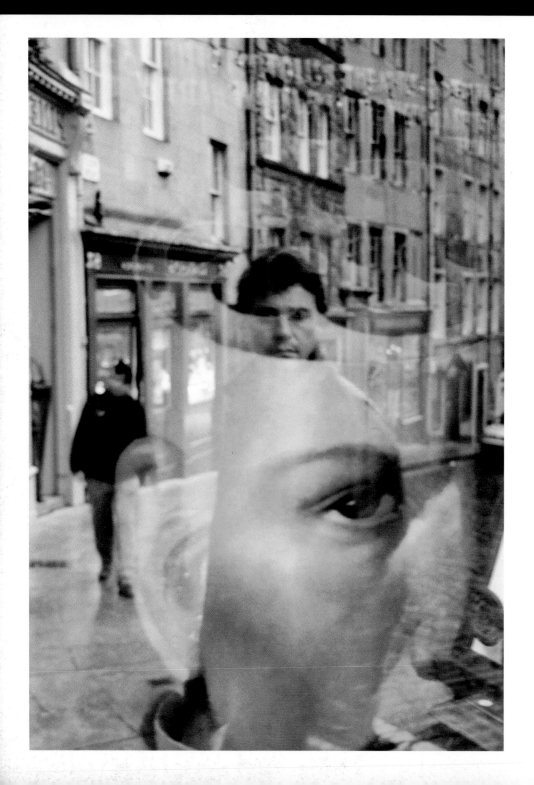

Developing your own view

Developing a personal style is important for every serious photographer, not just the professional. A good way to get started with discovering your own style is to pick a single subject and to try many different approaches to photographing it. Choosing one topic enables you to fully explore your subject matter and how it can be treated photographically.

A prestigious camera course in America once gave attendees only two sheets of handout notes. The first consisted of just three lines: 'One lens. One film. One developer.' The second read: 'Just take the picture.' This was a powerful way of bringing home the point to students that too many photographers lose out by not mastering their equipment. It is so easy to feel weighed down by camera features and technical options that you never get on with the picture-taking itself. To express yourself fluently with a camera – and that is what composition is all about – means that you must be so familiar with the equipment you can use it blindfold.

Beyond the initial outlay, digital cameras offer the photographer a no-cost option for experimentation – although, obviously, the bottom-range cameras may not offer sufficient technical control for a photographer to make informed choices. Compact digital cameras may be great for travelling and taking snapshots, but are more difficult to learn from. Digital SLRs offer better manual control – and, therefore, flexibility – but are considerably more expensive.

Starting out with a simple manual camera takes a lot of technical complexity out of the equation and allows you to get on with the creative process, to concentrate on the subject and on composition. This allows what you have to say to come through more clearly.

'The camera always points both ways. In expressing the subject, you also express yourself.'

Freeman Patterson (photographer)

Mind matters (facing opposite)

Mercedes Fages-Agudo began working with reflections while taking a photography class in Massachusetts. Shop-window reflections have since become a theme for her work. These images have featured in exhibitions and in the collaborative book *Second Storey*, which explored the appearance of buildings above street level in downtown Rochester, New York. This portrait of her partner was taken while attending a conference in Edinburgh. Turning to wait, his reflection in the shop window appears to be issuing from the head on the poster inside. The image was adopted as the publicity poster illustration for the sixth annual Photographer's Path exhibition at the High Falls Gallery in Rochester, New York.

Photographer: Mercedes Fages-Agudo.

Technical summary: Pentax ZX50 (US), 35–75mm zoom lens, Kodak Elitechrome 200.

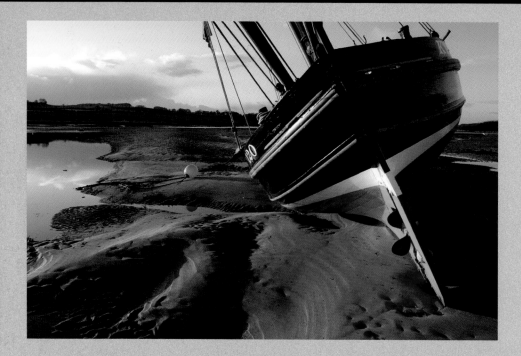

Final image, Alnmouth (above) and working the subject (below)

Working the subject from all angles to experiment with composition. Moving in line with the keel, the lower viewpoint and tighter crop on the boat provides the strongest composition. The form and texture of mud and hull are perfectly revealed – with rich reflected light from the hull.

Photographer: David Präkel.

Technical summary: 18 exposures in 11 minutes, final shot at 4.46pm. Nikon D100 with 18–35mm Zoom-Nikkor at 18mm, 1/160 sec at f6.7.

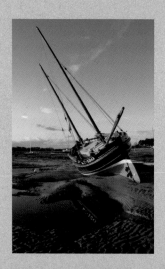
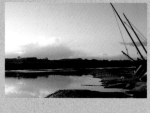
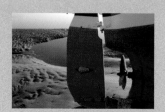
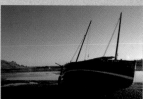
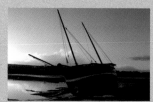

Explore, isolate, organise

It is all too easy to walk up to a photographic subject, lift the camera to the eye, press the shutter and hope to capture what you've seen. Ideally, you should know beforehand what you want the finished image to look like. Pre-visualisation underpins the act of composition.

Photographer and writer Andreas Feininger said that composition was a three-part process – exploration, isolation and organisation. You can prepare for your subject before you even touch a camera or reach the location. Preparation is key. If you already know what you intend to photograph, think around the subject in advance. From which angles would you photograph it? How will it change in different lights? How will you cope with movement? By thinking ahead in this way you can solve potential problems.

Exploration

Know what it is about the subject you want to say photographically. Bringing this idea to consciousness is vital as this will then drive your photographic vision. Exploration of the subject begins and continues with both eye and camera, looking for angles, viewpoints and at how the subject relates to potential backgrounds. If you can, take a range of preliminary images to explore your ideas – digital cameras are ideal for this.

Isolation

Isolation is the process of reducing your options to those that work best. Select the important aspects of the subject using techniques such as selective focusing and depth of field. The aim is to reduce visual clutter and confusion. Choice of lens, viewpoint – even materials – can do this. Once a potential exposure has been established, you can then choose the appropriate combination of shutter speed and aperture to favour either the appearance of motion or depth of field in the final image.

Organisation

Organisation is the process of choosing the frame and composing the arrangement of the elements within the frame to achieve the finished picture. This is the part of the process that most of us mean when we use the term 'composition'. However, without the important preliminaries of exploration and isolation this stage may produce a well-ordered image, but one that contains little that expresses your personal vision.

Working the subject

When you find your subject, work through the process of 'explore, isolate and organise' until you are happy with the result. By way of example, look at the images shown opposite, which follow this process of experimentation and selection. The texture of the estuary mud, the form of the boat hull, its crazy angle and the quality of late afternoon that was already fading – all conspired to catch my attention. Shooting from the shadow side of the hull produced lens flare and wasn't successful. A shot of close-up detail didn't work due to poor viewpoint – the white stripe on the boat hull merges into similarly toned water and there is poor lighting quality in the shadows. Tackling the shot from the other end of the boat was no better as the subject became lost in the poorly placed horizon line. Shooting reflections in the water pool was a good idea, but time was running out and the sun sinks quickly. The portrait format is acceptable, emphasising the angle of the masts, the light now beginning to fully reveal the form of the hull.

Humour

Psychoanalyst Sigmund Freud theorised that humour was 'the novel juxtaposition of two ideas'. Freud's definition offers photographers a way to create images that are teasingly ambiguous or out-and-out humorous. The choice of viewpoint and picture-taking angle can often align two objects that may seem innocuous separately, but absurd together. This trick is a favourite of press photographers. At political rallies and conferences they often frame the speaker against part of a party slogan or logo – the press photographer's equivalent of aligning some poor unsuspecting individual with the stag's head on the wall so they appear to have 'grown' a pair of antlers. This approach exploits the spatial possibilities of the photographer's art to humorous ends.

Equally productive for the photographer are opportunities to play with time. Just as we love to solve the puzzle of images with more than one meaning, we take special pleasure in freezing an amusing instance in a single image – what would be considered a 'sight gag' in cinema or on stage. Because of its ability to freeze time, photography can create an enduring joke, in which the inevitable threatens, but never happens; where the visual 'punch line' is hinted at, but never delivered.

It is a challenge to consciously create successful humorous images – the images tend to find the receptive photographer rather than the other way around. For photographers, humour, like fortune, favours the prepared mind.

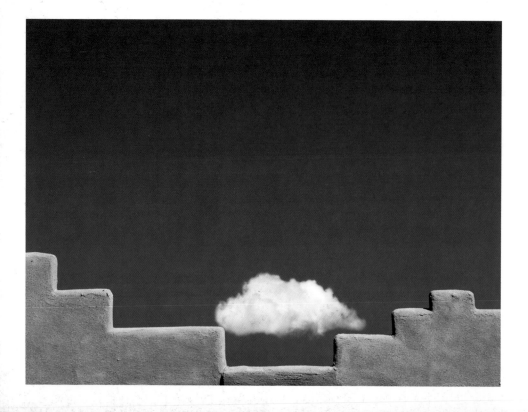

Cloud supporter (facing opposite)

Two simple subjects, such as a wall and a cloud, can be aligned so that the cloud appears to rest on the wall for a while. It is not a 'belly laugh' of a joke – nor is it intended to be – but you cannot help but smile every time you see such an image.

Photographer: Todd Laffler.

Technical summary: Sony Cybershot DSC-F717, 1/125 sec at f8.

One Way – San Fransisco, 2001 (below)

An example of Freud's 'novel juxtaposition'. The viewpoint juxtaposes the traffic sign with the religious statue. The dramatic lighting adds to the sense that the sign is directing 'lost souls'.

Photographer: Adam Moore.

Technical summary: Hasselblad 501CM with 80mm Zeiss lens, 5 minutes at f4, Kodak TMax 100 developed in Agfa Rodinal. Sepia-toned, silver halide print with some edge burning.

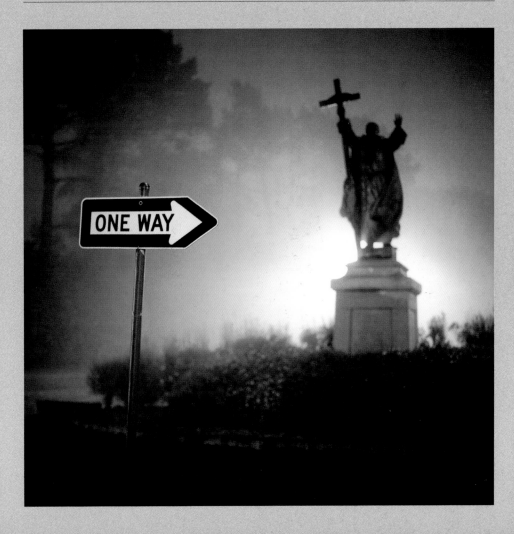

Contrasts

The Bauhaus movement in 1920s Germany taught that an image that captures and holds the attention must contain a dynamic based on contrast or contrasts. For many, 'contrast' in photography means black and white or dark and light, but there are many alternative ways in which the subject can contrast with the background, or for there to be contrasts within the subject itself.

Photographers learn to exploit difference. The strongest contrast is between a dark shape and a light background or vice versa. However, beyond contrast of tone, there are contrasts of orientation or texture. Select viewpoint and lighting that will reveal these differences in your images.

Ideas about contrast in photography evolved out of colour theories developed by painter and art theoretician Johannes Itten, who taught at the Bauhaus. Itten's theories of contrasts, colour and form were developed to give art and design students a feeling for materials. The theories were also applied in the Bauhaus approach to photography. Students were given a list of 'contrasts' and were initially asked to produce pairs of photographs that contrasted with each other. The second, more difficult, stage of the exercise was to combine the contrasting elements in just one image.

The list, below, is similar to that studied by the Bauhaus photographers. It can be used as a mental exercise to imagine how to incorporate these contrasts into images or it can be used as a basis for creating real images. Some examples are quite straightforward, others more abstract and conceptual. The idea of incorporating contrast into images is not just applicable to fine art photography, but to all genres of the subject. Contrasts can be incorporated into every picture you make to create energy and dynamism. As the Bauhaus list suggests, all the formal elements can be opposed and used dynamically; photographic aspects such as focus or the appearance of motion can be contrasted in this way too.

point – line	large – small	diagonal – circular	rough – smooth
area – line	long – short	straight – curved	hard – soft
line – body	broad – narrow	round – square	heavy – light
area – body	much – little	horizontal – vertical	strong – weak
	many – few	high – low	
still – moving	light – dark	liquid – solid	
continuous – intermittent	black – white	pointed – blunt	
	transparent – opaque	loud – soft	

List of contrast pairs.

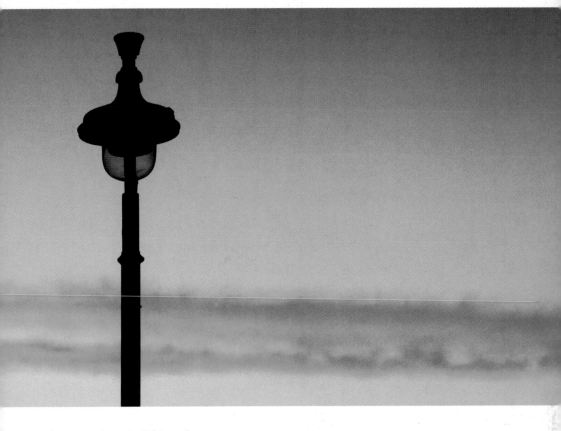

Lamp and contrail (above)
In terms of form, colour and orientation, the silhouetted unlit lamp confronts the aircraft condensation trail left across the sky. The soft, pink glow of a setting sun offers contrast in a city sky.

Photographer: David Präkel.

Technical summary: Leica R4, 180mm Elmarit, Ektachrome 200 Pro.

'Exaggeration is a vital ingredient of art.'

(unattributed)

Imbalance

Photographers can choose to shake up their compositions by intentionally breaking the 'rules' of composition and creating an imbalance in their images. For some, focusing beyond the subject and cropping the subject in an extreme way are techniques that can shift the balance of an image and unsettle the viewer.

Unusual and challenging perspectives are afforded by using a super wide-angle, fish-eye or extreme telephoto lens, though the profusion of this kind of image in the media does serve to lessen their impact. This means that photographers have to work harder to find new angles – for example, looking for a viewpoint and angle that disorientates the viewer. Such effects work best if they are exaggerated, so experiment and be bold.

Landscape photographers can disorientate the viewer by removing the horizon from the image, which takes away the usual frame of reference. Making an extreme close-up will abstract the image and reduce the subject to graphic representation. This can be disturbing as it removes all reference to scale.

In terms of colour, fashion photographers long ago began to experiment with the viewer's expectation by cross-processing their films, producing bizarre, but consistent colour shifts throughout their images. Cross-processing involves developing a colour film in the wrong chemistry. Digitally, these effects are now quite straightforward to imitate without resorting to chemical effects – it also means you can have a 'straight' version of your image without sacrificing the original.

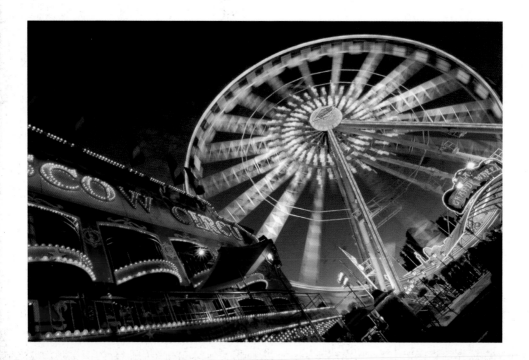

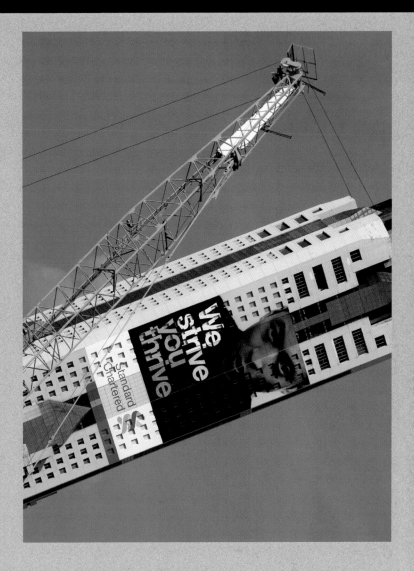

La Grande Wheel (facing opposite)

A long exposure captures the lights and movement of the Ferris wheel. The excitement of the fairground is perfectly encapsulated.

Photographer: Bill Taylor.

Technical summary: Nikon D70, 12mm lens, 1/2 sec at f22, ISO 200.

Skyscraper (above)

The diagonals and the 'falling' tower block give the viewer the impression that disaster is imminent. The picture imitates the dizzying effect you get putting your head back and turning round to look at the buildings above you in the city.

Photographer: Wilson Tsoi.

Technical summary: Nikon D70 Nikkor 80–200mm f2.8 AF-D, 1/800 sec at f8, ISO 200.

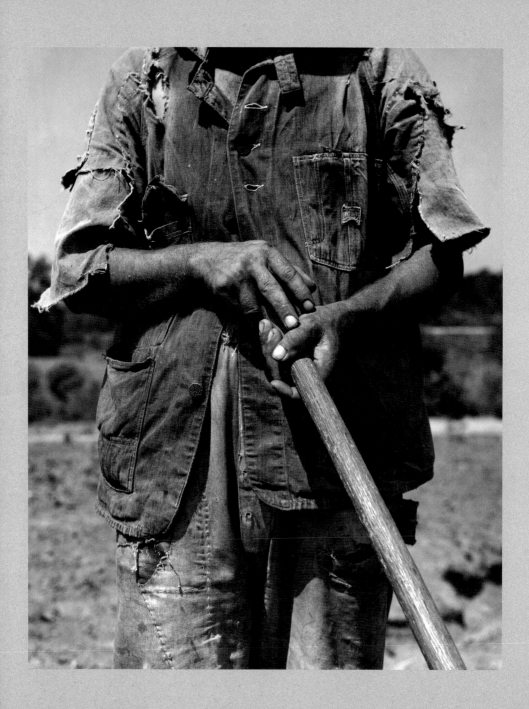

Cropping

In 'Size in the frame' (page 98), we looked at subject placement, cropping and the importance of composing in-camera. Some photographers find it difficult to compose in-camera. While the process has many advantages, there are times when it is best to finesse the crop after the image has been taken. Strong cropping can make an image.

There are two major considerations when cropping. The first is the form of the final image frame; it is worth keeping in mind the proportion of the image when choosing a crop. Of course, this should not prevent you from creating severely cropped images if appropriate to the subject matter and the final presentation. For prints, a pair of good cropping 'ells' with dimensions marked on one side helps. You can cut your own ells from black card. Computer cropping to a target aspect ratio (and resolution) is very straightforward. Image-editing software now permits free rotation of the Crop box, which can be used to either square up a wayward horizon or to produce a completely new slant on the image.

There is no reason to choose rectangular or square frames when cropping – an asymmetrical crop can create a complete shift in emphasis. Try a trapezoid so that only two sides of the rectangle are parallel. American photographer Robert Heinecken produced puzzle images from sections of cropped prints. Circles and ellipses tend to look dated, as can the soft-edged 'vignette'. It is easy to control these effects digitally and it is well worth experimenting with the technique on certain subjects.

A second consideration concerns the placement of the subject in the new image. You can locate the point of interest with mathematical precision, but ideally you should trust your visual instincts and crop around the subject in a way that seems to you to visually 'fit'. If the image is important, mark the crop temporarily with black paper and try living with the cropped image for a while to judge the effect.

Tidying up

The most minimal cropping of an image is still worthwhile, for example to tidy up or remove distracting or intrusive elements from the edge of the frame – often these are invisible during the picture-taking, particularly with a camera that does not show 100 per cent of the view. If the print is for exhibition, cutting a slightly smaller window in the overlay mat does this form of cropping most effectively.

Hoe culture (left)

This iconic image of a poor cotton worker was achieved by deliberate hard cropping in-camera to exclude the head. We pay more attention to the clothes and the worker's hands in the absence of the subject's facial features. The hands become the subject's identifying feature, through which the narrative of the subject's life is told. The crop around the subject enables the viewer to interpret not simply the hardship of the individual, but of all migrant workers.

Photographer: Dorothea Lange.

Technical summary: None provided.

Colour

As one of the key elements of composition, pure colour is a
subject worthy of exploration in its own right. Colour provides
a rich source of opportunity for the photographer, with its
strong associations with moods. However, colour is difficult
to capture without introducing secondary compositional
elements such as shape, texture or form. The truly abstract
colour image is hard to find in the real world, and it is a
challenging exercise to photograph something to leave
only colour. De-focusing the lens will abstract the image to
some extent, though it still requires some careful composition
to isolate the colour from its environment. Garden flowers
and indoor plants are a great source for this kind of colour
composition.

Skies make a perfect subject for abstract colour images.
Although the colour range is wide and rich, it will never
include certain portions of the colour wheel. With skies,
you can be certain that your images will be completely
original. Water and reflections offer a wider range of colours,
but can be surprisingly difficult to capture successfully with
good image sharpness; the water surface is usually much
closer than the reflections in it appear to be. (The same
problem occurs when photographing a mirror – you can focus
on the frame or the refection, but not both.) To achieve this,
you require a small aperture, which means using a longer
shutter speed, and this risks a little image movement.
However, encountering and solving problems of this kind
is part of the enjoyment.

Once you have tackled an obvious source of colour, it
becomes easier (and somewhat addictive) to source these
interesting qualities in more unusual subjects, such as lichen
on a stone wall, which displays an unexpected array of
colours – or in the colour of the stone itself. A personal
favourite is weathered and peeling paint, which can be
found in all kinds of locations – from the boats moored
on the quayside of fishing villages to the distressed walls of
old cottages.

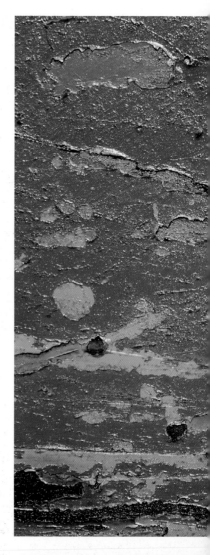

Rust (below)

This looks like a landscape. The reality: it is an oil-soaked, rusting engine cover on an excavator. A loose chain has scarred the surface, breaking through the new paint to the ancient colours beneath.

Photographer: David Präkel.

Technical summary: Nikon D100 with 60mm Micro-Nikkor, 1/200 sec at f8.

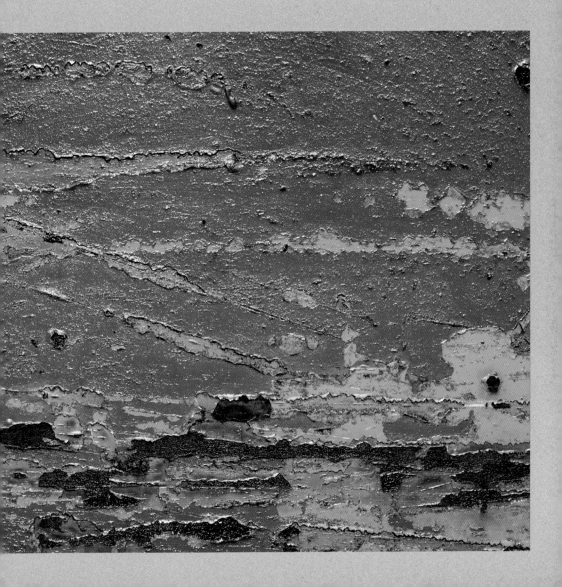

Digital imaging

The introduction of digital technology to photography has, without doubt, transformed it for ever. On the one hand, it offers unlimited scope for image-correction and enhancement, as well as experimentation with composition, montage and other special effects. Once in the digital domain, image data becomes completely manipulable. The possibilities are limited only by imagination. On the other hand, conventional photography has suffered somewhat. The impact of digital on technological development for the consumer has meant that film-based companies have axed product ranges or simply gone out of business, which has affected the range of choice for traditional photographers. This is essentially a practical matter, but digital also impacts directly on composition in terms of pre-visualisation. By shifting the emphasis away from capture to post-production it can encourage photographers to rely on a quick-fix approach to image-making, rather than perfecting their skills in-camera. Without wishing to denigrate digital entirely, the ease with which photographers can now manipulate natural and other phenomena – sunsets, for example – has debased the natural effects that can be captured in the moment in-camera. Photographers now present composite landscapes where skies have been dropped in to look 'real'. Heavily stylised images increasingly replace well-composed ones, and we are in danger of forgetting what the real world looks like. It is worth keeping these concerns in mind for your own photography. What kinds of effects are you after? How authentic do you want your photography to be?

On balance, however, digital imaging gives photographers an ideal opportunity to experiment. This is not the same as taking as many images as possible simply to see 'what comes out'. Experimentation is about setting up an idea beforehand, exploring a particular approach and evaluating the results against the original idea. Unexpected discoveries and chance may change the course of the experiment. Unlike film, digital offers photographers the opportunity to instantly review and assess the results at no cost. The same applies to digital post-production work – until you make a print, there is no outlay.

Unique digital features include the History Brush that enables previous layers of image adjustment to be painted back into the master image. The sophistication of blurring and sharpening techniques enables you to improve the quality of the lens-created image. Colorisation techniques mean that digital toning need not be limited to imitations of the chemical processes.

The potential for digital in the future is exciting. One such development is High Dynamic Range (or HDR) images, which more accurately represent the range of brightness we perceive in the real world. By combining a series of exposures, an HDR image can record both the shadow detail and highlights that neither digital sensors nor film has previously been able to resolve. This can free up photographers from conventional restraints on composition imposed by lighting or picture-taking angle and offer opportunities to 're-expose' the image after the fact. HDR images are especially suited to photographs of room interiors that contain a view through a window or doorway of the brightly lit outdoors – in fact, any scene with an extreme brightness range. The only consideration is movement. With an image composed of up to 12 exposures, the photographer must be aware of potential movement in the image.

Digital alternatives to a traditional technique

Silkscreen printing offers photographers a way to simplify the composition of images to a few graphic shapes and tones, each of which is printed in a solid ink colour through a mesh screen. It requires skill and the right equipment that, for some, may not be a worthy investment. The results can mean loss of image detail, but the boldness is impressive.

Image-editing software offers a similar technique that can retain fine detail. The starting point is a black-and-white image with strong, graphic shapes and a full range of tones. The Threshold command is used to create a series of bitmap images representing the aggregate tones of the image. The resulting 1-bit bitmap stores only black or white information. The three images can then be 'colorised' through the Hue/Saturation and Lightness command and printed in solid colours in three passes through a printer. Slight mis-registration between the colours can be an unexpected bonus, which you have to fight hard to achieve with the reproduction accuracy of modern ink-jet printers.

Filling station (below)

This is an old filling station in the far north of England, composed of three colours selected by personal associations with the colours of fuel company logos and rust – in other words, the colour elements missing from the original monochrome image.

Photographer: David Präkel.

Technical summary: Nikon FE with Nikon 50mm F1.4, Ilford FP4 Plus.

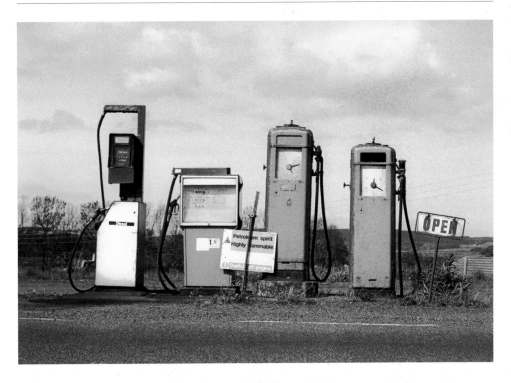

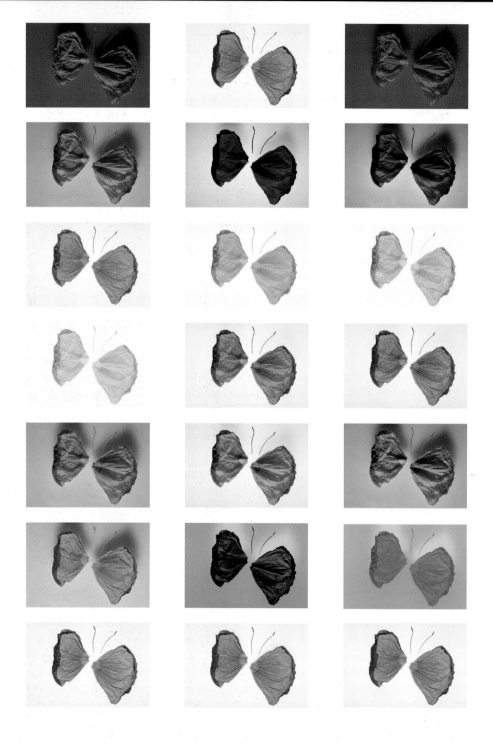

Unique digital techniques

Typology of the butterflower: this image came about by happenstance. The petals and stamens from a yellow flower in the studio had dropped, and the pattern they formed was evocative of the shape of a butterfly. This pattern was recreated on a light box and two digital exposures were made: one with top lighting and one with transmitted light. The top lighting was directed to cast a shadow above the butterflower, like an over-wintering butterfly found by torchlight high up on a wall. The intention was to blend the two digital images as Photoshop layers in a single image to reveal both the delicacy and translucency of the dying petals and their form and texture from the top 'shadow' lighting.

The range of final images that resulted from using different blending modes and adjusting the opacity of the top layer brought to mind the subsequent presentation. The profusion of images suggested a typology (a study of types) of this imaginary butterflower in a presentation, echoing Victorian specimen boxes. The original two images are included in the top row and other blended images arranged in a manner appropriate to their density. The resulting piece represents just a few of the many techniques that can be performed in the world of digital imaging. Unlike real butterflies collected for their endless variation, here the 'specimens' are superficially different, though the content of the images is in fact identical; they are clones.

Typology (left)

First image, top row: natural light; second image, top row: transmitted light; all other images are combinations of these two using Photoshop layers and blending modes.

Photographer: David Präkel.

Technical summary: Nikon D100 60mm Micro-Nikkor, 1/4 sec at f8 and 1/90 sec at f8, ISO 200.

Conclusion ▷

To summarise: before composing a picture, first compose your own thoughts. Finding a moment to reflect on the subject – to be true to the emotions it produces in you – will inform your photography. A calligrapher may spend many hours in preparation before executing one character that seems to have been produced in an instant. This process of contemplation and execution is very similar to that of composition in photography.

At first, the process of composition appears to be cumbersome. It takes conscious effort and time. Many photographers find this puts a brake on spontaneous picture-taking, so they give up on composition, hoping that inspiration will somehow show them favour. However, quality picture-making requires much more than chance. Good composition comes about through developing an eye and experience.

By persevering with an analysis of every image-making opportunity, by identifying each of the formal elements and then weighing the importance of each against your own intentions, the process will eventually become automatic. You will soon become unaware of the process itself and begin to find your responses to your subject more immediate and successful.

How is this achieved? Look at lots of images by other photographers and observe the way in which they use the elements of composition. But most of all, it's achieved by experimenting with each of the elements, singly and in combination (colour and shape or form and texture, for example), and by reminding yourself that the principles of composition can be adapted to fuel your own creative expression, without limits. Learn the rules, and then learn how to bend them.

Finally, always ask: 'Why am I photographing this?' The answer will inform your image-making and improve your pictures. The more images you make and the more images you look at, the more composition will become a natural part of your picture-taking and will, in the end, look after itself.

Jim Allen
www.differenthats.com

Nina Indset Andersen
www.eyesondesign.net

John Barclay
www.barclayphoto.com

Markos Berndt
www.markosphoto.com

Harry Callahan
www.pacemacgill.com

Marina Cano
www.marinacano.com
www.photo.net/photos/
Marina%20Cano

Henri Cartier-Bresson
www.magnumphotos.com

Jorge Coimbra
www.jorgecoimbra.home.sapo.pt

Stephen Coll
stephen@coll1469.freeserve.co.uk

John Darwell
www.johndarwell.com

Pat di Fruscia
www.difrusciaphotography.com

Alec Ee
www.photo.net/photos/alecee
www.pbase.com/alecee
www.photo4me.com

David Elsworth
d_elsworth@yahoo.co.u

Tiago Estima
www.estima.home.sapo.pt

Karl Facredyn
www.tangerineglow.com

Mercedes Fages-Agudo
www.geocities.com/merche_fages/

Sam Henderson
www.cumbria.ac.uk

David Hockney
Richard Gray
www.richardgraygallery.com

Eric Kellerman
www.erickellermanphotography.com

Brad Kim
byong_ho_kim@yahoo.com

Todd Laffler
www.toddlaffler.com

Dorothea Lange
www.museumca.org

Caroline Leeming
cazleeming@hotmail.com

Marion Luijten
www.coloursofnature.com

Tom McGhee
Trevillion Images
www.tommcgheephoto.com
www.trevillion.com

Karen Melvin
www.karenmelvin.com

Duane Michals
www.pacemacgill.com

Jean-Sébastien Monzani
www.jsmonzani.com

Adam Moore
www.adammoore.com

James Nachtwey
www.jamesnachtwey.com
www.viiphoto.com

Martin Parr
www.magnumphotos.com

David Prakel/
PhotoWorkshops Partnership
www.photopartners.co.uk
david@photopartners.co.uk

Cindy Quinn
www.quinnimages.com

Bjorn Rannestad
www.rannestadphotos.com

Marc Riboud
www.magnumphotos.com

Felipe Rodriguez
www.beatusille.net

Tomas Rucker
www.trman.wz.cz

Trine Sirnes Thorne
www.sirnesphotography.com

Nana Sousa Dias
www.nanasousadias.com

Paul Stefan
www.paulstefanphotography.com

Kevin Summers
www.kevinsummersphotography.com

Mellik Tamas
www.melliktamas.com

Bill Taylor
www.pbase.com/billphoto

Michael Trevillion
Trevillion Images
www.trevillion.com

Wilson Tsoi
www.photo.net/photos/wilsontsoi

Ilona Wellmann
www.ilonawellmann.meinatelier.de

Sotiris Zafeiris
www.sotiriszafeiris.com

Achromatic
Neutral or without colour.

Aesthetic(s)
Philosophical theory of what is beautiful; pleasing in appearance.

Ambient light
Available or existing light.

Analogue photography
Film and chemical photography, often called 'wet' photography as opposed to digital.

Aperture
Variable opening in the lens that controls the amount of light reaching the film or sensor.

Aspect ratio
The ratio of the width of an image to its height.

Bracketing
Intentional over- and underexposure from the indicated exposure, usually in whole or half stops.

Camera obscura
Darkened room with a small aperture that projects an inverted image of outside world on to opposite wall. Origins of the word 'camera'.

Catchlight
Bright reflection in the eyes of the subject in a portrait.

Closure
Making whole a shape or form that is only suggested.

Colour cast
Unwanted, overall colour change in an image.

Colour temperature
Measure of 'whiteness' of light, measured in Kelvin (see White balance).

Complementary colours
Diametrically opposite colours on the colour wheel.

Concerned photography
Documentary photography with a social or political agenda.

Construct
A general idea resulting from systematic thinking.

Contrast
Difference in brightness between the darkest and lightest parts of the image.

Contrast curve
Image editing software tool that allows selective adjustments of tones and overall contrast.

De-focus
Intentionally blur an image by putting the image-forming lens out of focus.

Depth of field
Apparent sharpness in front and behind exact point of focus; varies with format, aperture and focusing distance.

Desaturate/Saturate
Decrease/increase the strength of all colours.

Diffuse lighting
Scattered, spread out, light; not concentrated in one place.

Digital imaging
Images created by sampling where brightness or colour are stored in binary number code.

D-SLR
Digital single lens reflex camera.

Exposure
Combination of intensity and duration of light used to allow the right amount of light to reach film or sensor to record full tonal range.

Fast
Lens with great light gathering ability. Film that reacts quickly to light (usually coarse grained). High ISO number.

Figure work
Photography involving the clothed and unclothed human form.

Film grain
Appearance in the final image of the individual specs of silver salt that make up the tones of the picture (see Noise).

Film speed
Measure of film's sensitivity to light (see ISO).

Filter
Glass or plastic device that modifies light passing through the camera lens. Computer software module that applies image effect .

Flare
Non image-forming, unwanted light in a photographic image often formed by reflection on the glass elements of the lens itself.

Focal length
Measure of field of view of a lens; technically, the distance between the optical centre of the lens and the focused image for a subject at infinity.

f-stop
Diameter of the lens opening represented as a fraction of the focal length. The bigger the f number, the smaller the opening.

Graduated filter
Partly-toned resin or plastic filter with slightly more than half of the filter clear. Clear to grey area has a smooth transition. Used to darken skies or control contrast.

Grey card
Standard piece of card that reflects 18 percent of the light falling on it to provide an exact mid-tone light reading.

Hard light
Strongly directional light that creates high contrast.

Histogram
A bar chart of frequency distribution showing how many pixels are found at each brightness level.

Hyperfocal distance/Hyperfocal focus
Closest focused point at which the far end of the depth of field stretches to infinity; focusing to achieve greatest depth of field.

Incident light
Light falling on the subject.

Incident light meter (hand-held meter)
Device which measures the power of the light falling on the subject (see Reflected light meter).

Iris
Metal blades that create variable aperture in lens.

ISO/ISO number
International Organisation for Standardisation – body that sets standard for film speeds and matching digital sensitivity.

Joiner
Term coined by artist David Hockney to describe his photographic collages.

Kelvin
Unit of measurement for colour temperature – not degrees Kelvin.

Latitude
Degree of over- and underexposure film or digital sensor can accommodate and still provide an acceptable image.

Light
Spectrum of electro-magnetic radiation visible to the human eye bounded by ultra violet (UV) and infrared (IR).

Light meter/Exposure meter
Measures intensity of light for photography, giving value as a combination of shutter speed and aperture or a single Exposure Value (EV) number for a given film speed or sensitivity.

Mat
Card overlay that creates a border to a framed print.

Maximum aperture
Biggest possible aperture when lens is 'fully open'; least depth of field.

Minimum aperture
Smallest aperture (biggest f number) when lens is said to be 'stopped down'; greatest depth of field.

Monochromatic
Single colour, usually meaning black and white.

MPx (megapixel)
Million pixels – measure of digital camera resolution.

ND
Neutral density filter that reduces light intensity equally across spectrum.

Noise
Out-of-place pixels that break up flat tones in a digital image. Either colour (chroma) noise or luminance (luma) noise or a combination.

Normal lens/Standard lens
Lens of certain focal length, varying with the format (e.g. 50mm for 35mm film), which gives closest perspective to 'normal' vision in a 10x8 inch print held at arm's length.

Open up
Let more light through a lens by changing iris to create a bigger aperture (smaller f number) (see Stop down).

Overexposure
Images created with too much light, having no shadows or dark tones (see Underexposure).

Palette
An assortment or range of colours.

Panning
Camera moves with moving subject to create sharp image of subject against blurred background.

Panoramic
Very wide view as seen from a great distance. Wide aspect ratio format (2:1 or greater) or camera taking wide images.

Photosensitive
Reacts to visible light.

Pinhole camera
Simple, lens-less camera where image is made by light entering through a tiny hole the size of a pin prick.

Pixel
Digital picture element.

Polariser/Polarising filter
Used over lens to control reflections from non-metallic surfaces and to darken skies at 90 degrees to the sun.

Portrait lens
Lens with a focal length that gives flattering proportions to an image of the face.

Post-processing
Image manipulation after print has been made.

Pre-visualise
Imagining how the finished image will look before an exposure is made.

Prime lens
Single focal length lens, often better quality or faster than a zoom.

Raking light
Light falling across subject at a shallow angle, which reveals texture.

Rangefinder
Direct vision viewfinder with superimposed images from secondary window to affect focusing; camera that uses same (see Viewfinder).

Reflected light meter
Common light meter in cameras that measures light reflected by subject and therefore influenced by reflective quality of subject.

Selective focus
Choosing carefully where the plane of focus falls in the image.

Sepia tone
A brown tone associated with early photographic images.

Shutter
Device that controls the time for which the film or sensor is exposed.

Shutter speed
The time for which the film or sensor is exposed when a picture is taken.

Silver gelatin
Conventional black and white photographic print on fibre paper, named after image-forming gelatin layer with photosensitive silver salts.

Slow
Lens with limited light gathering ability. Film that reacts slowly to light (usually fine grained). Low ISO number.

SLR (Single-lens reflex)
Camera using a mirror to show photographer what the taking lens 'sees'. View blacks out during exposure (see TLR).

Soft light
Diffuse light that gives few shadows.

Split-toned
Use of different colours or degrees of toning in highlights and shadow of a print.

Static
Fixed, unmoving or unchanging.

Stop
Photographer's unit used to express ratios of light or exposure. One stop is a doubling or halving. ISO film speeds, standard apertures and shutter speeds can be expressed in stops.

Stop down
Let less light through a lens by changing iris to create a smaller aperture (bigger f number) (see Open up).

Straight print
Unaltered version of image.

Telephoto
Long focal length lens, makes distant objects appear closer.

TLR (Twin-lens reflex)
Camera using a second lens and a mirror to show what is being photographed. Making an exposure does not affect view (see SLR).

Tonality
Quality of tone or contrast.

Tone
Full range of greys from solid black to pure white.

Toning
Chemically or digitally altering neutral grey tones. Brown, yellow or red-greys give 'warm' look, while blue tones look 'cold'. Archival treatment of silver gelatin prints.

TTL (Through the Lens)
Reflected light meter in cameras that measures light through the taking lens.

Tungsten light
Light produced by incandescent (glowing) light bulbs from domestic bulbs (2900K) to studio tungsten lights (3200K).

Underexposure
Images created with too little light, no highlights or light tones (see Overexposure).

View camera
Large format bellows camera with total freedom of movement of lens and film planes, which means perspective and depth of field can be controlled independently of aperture.

Viewfinder
Direct vision optical framing device; camera that uses same (see Rangefinder).

Viewpoint
Place in space where the camera/observer is positioned – determines perspective.

Vignette
Image with no distinct border but which gradually fades into the background.

White balance
Adjust for the colour temperature of the illuminating light so white and neutral colours appear truly neutral and do not have a colour cast.

White light
Equal blend of all colours in visible spectrum.

Wide-angle
Lens with wide field of view, also super wide and ultra wide.

Working aperture
Chosen aperture for a particular exposure.

Zoom
Lens with variable focal length.

I would like to acknowledge the debt owed to Alan J. Lefley who taught me a great deal about photography and design while never formally being my teacher. Thanks are due also to staff and members of the Community Darkroom in Rochester, NY, without whose encouragement and support I would not be teaching photography.

For this book: thanks to all those who have generously contributed ideas and images, especially my colleagues at the Cumbria Institute of the Arts, in particular Mike England (course leader BA Hons Photography); Sam Henderson (photography lecturer) and John Darwell (part-time lecturer). To my students who have always given me at least as many ideas as I have given them. Finally, thanks to my wife Alison: your role as sounding board and proofreader should never be underestimated.

CREDITS

Cover: Nina Indset Andersen

Page 51: © The Estate of Harry Callahan. Courtesy Pace/MacGill, New York

Page 53: From work published by Alfred L. Yarbus, Eye Movements and Vision, Plenum Press, New York (1967)

Page 64: Ian Washing His Hair, London, January, 1983. 1983 photographic collage, edition: 15. 30x33" © David Hockney

Page 85: © Martin Parr / Magnum

Page 101: © Henri Cartier-Bresson / Magnum

Page 111: © Marc Riboud / Magnum

Page 131: © Henri Cartier-Bresson / Magnum

Page 132: © Duane Michals. Courtesy Pace/MacGill, New York

Page 150: Kevin Summers Photography

Page 153: © 2005 JS Monzani

Page 159: © toddlaffler.com

Page 164: Hoe Culture, near Anniston, Alabama, 1936 by Dorothea Lange © Library of Congress, Prints & Photographs Division, FSA/OWI Collection, LC-USZ6-1028

BASICS
PHOTOGRAPHY

Working with ethics

Lynne Elvins
Naomi Goulder

Publisher's note

The subject of ethics is not new, yet its consideration within the applied visual arts is perhaps not as prevalent as it might be. Our aim here is to help a new generation of students, educators and practitioners find a methodology for structuring their thoughts and reflections in this vital area.

AVA Publishing hopes that these **Working with ethics** pages provide a platform for consideration and a flexible method for incorporating ethical concerns in the work of educators, students and professionals. Our approach consists of four parts:

The **introduction** is intended to be an accessible snapshot of the ethical landscape, both in terms of historical development and current dominant themes.

The **framework** positions ethical consideration into four areas and poses questions about the practical implications that might occur. Marking your response to each of these questions on the scale shown will allow your reactions to be further explored by comparison.

The **case study** sets out a real project and then poses some ethical questions for further consideration. This is a focus point for a debate rather than a critical analysis so there are no predetermined right or wrong answers.

A selection of **further reading** for you to consider areas of particular interest in more detail.

Ethical: aware-
ness/
reflect-
ion/
debate

Working with ethics

Introduction

Ethics is a complex subject that interlaces the idea of responsibilities to society with a wide range of considerations relevant to the character and happiness of the individual. It concerns virtues of compassion, loyalty and strength, but also of confidence, imagination, humour and optimism. As introduced in ancient Greek philosophy, the fundamental ethical question is: *what should I do?* How we might pursue a 'good' life not only raises moral concerns about the effects of our actions on others, but also personal concerns about our own integrity.

In modern times the most important and controversial questions in ethics have been the moral ones. With growing populations and improvements in mobility and communications, it is not surprising that considerations about how to structure our lives together on the planet should come to the forefront. For visual artists and communicators, it should be no surprise that these considerations will enter into the creative process.

Some ethical considerations are already enshrined in government laws and regulations or in professional codes of conduct. For example, plagiarism and breaches of confidentiality can be punishable offences. Legislation in various nations makes it unlawful to exclude people with disabilities from accessing information or spaces. The trade of ivory as a material has been banned in many countries. In these cases, a clear line has been drawn under what is unacceptable.

But most ethical matters remain open to debate, among experts and lay-people alike, and in the end we have to make our own choices on the basis of our own guiding principles or values. Is it more ethical to work for a charity than for a commercial company? Is it unethical to create something that others find ugly or offensive?

Specific questions such as these may lead to other questions that are more abstract. For example, is it only effects on humans (and what they care about) that are important, or might effects on the natural world require attention too?

Is promoting ethical consequences justified even when it requires ethical sacrifices along the way? Must there be a single unifying theory of ethics (such as the Utilitarian thesis that the right course of action is always the one that leads to the greatest happiness of the greatest number), or might there always be many different ethical values that pull a person in various directions?

As we enter into ethical debate and engage with these dilemmas on a personal and professional level, we may change our views or change our view of others. The real test though is whether, as we reflect on these matters, we change the way we act as well as the way we think. Socrates, the 'father' of philosophy, proposed that people will naturally do 'good' if they know what is right. But this point might only lead us to yet another question: *how do we know what is right?*

Working with ethics

You
What are your ethical beliefs?

Central to everything you do will be your attitude to people and issues around you. For some people, their ethics are an active part of the decisions they make every day as a consumer, a voter or a working professional. Others may think about ethics very little and yet this does not automatically make them unethical. Personal beliefs, lifestyle, politics, nationality, religion, gender, class or education can all influence your ethical viewpoint.

Using the scale, where would you place yourself? What do you take into account to make your decision? Compare results with your friends or colleagues.

Your client
What are your terms?

Working relationships are central to whether ethics can be embedded into a project, and your conduct on a day-to-day basis is a demonstration of your professional ethics. The decision with the biggest impact is whom you choose to work with in the first place. Cigarette companies or arms traders are often-cited examples when talking about where a line might be drawn, but rarely are real situations so extreme. At what point might you turn down a project on ethical grounds and how much does the reality of having to earn a living affect your ability to choose?

Using the scale, where would you place a project? How does this compare to your personal ethical level?

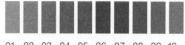
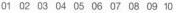

01 02 03 04 05 06 07 08 09 10

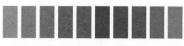

01 02 03 04 05 06 07 08 09 10

Your specifications
What are the impacts of your materials?

In relatively recent times, we are learning that many natural materials are in short supply. At the same time, we are increasingly aware that some man-made materials can have harmful, long-term effects on people or the planet. How much do you know about the materials that you use? Do you know where they come from, how far they travel and under what conditions they are obtained? When your creation is no longer needed, will it be easy and safe to recycle? Will it disappear without a trace? Are these considerations your responsibility or are they out of your hands?

Using the scale, mark how ethical your material choices are.

Your creation
What is the purpose of your work?

Between you, your colleagues and an agreed brief, what will your creation achieve? What purpose will it have in society and will it make a positive contribution? Should your work result in more than commercial success or industry awards? Might your creation help save lives, educate, protect or inspire? Form and function are two established aspects of judging a creation, but there is little consensus on the obligations of visual artists and communicators toward society, or the role they might have in solving social or environmental problems. If you want recognition for being the creator, how responsible are you for what you create and where might that responsibility end?

Using the scale, mark how ethical the purpose of your work is.

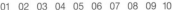

01 02 03 04 05 06 07 08 09 10

01 02 03 04 05 06 07 08 09 10

Working with ethics

One aspect of photography that raises an ethical dilemma is that of inherent truth or untruth in manipulating images, particularly with the use of digital cameras. Photographs have, arguably, always been manipulated and at best they represent the subjective view of the photographer in one moment of time. There has always been darkroom manipulation through retouching or double exposures, but these effects are far easier to produce digitally and harder to detect. In the past, the negative was physical evidence of the original, but digital cameras don't leave similar tracks.

While creative photography might not set out to capture and portray images with the same intent that documentary photography might, is there an inherent deception in making food look tastier, people appear better looking or resorts look more spacious and attractive? Does commercial image manipulation of this kind set out to favour the content in order to please, or is it contrary to public interest if it results in a purchase based on a photograph that was never 'the real thing'? How much responsibility should a photographer have when the more real alternative might not sell?

Bernarr Macfadden's *New York Evening Graphic* was dubbed 'the Porno Graphic' for its emphasis on sex, gossip and crime news. In the early 1920s, Macfadden had set out to break new ground and publish a newspaper that would speak the language of the average person. One of the paper's trademark features was the creation and use of the composograph. These were often scandalous photographic images that were made using retouched photo collages doctored to imply real situations. The most notorious use of the composograph was for the sensational Rhinelander divorce trial in 1925.

Wealthy New York socialite Leonard Kip Rhinelander married Alice Jones, a nursemaid and laundress he had fallen in love with. When word got out, it was one of high society's most shocking public scandals in generations. Not only was Alice a common maid, it was also revealed that her father was African American. After six weeks of pressure from his family, Rhinelander sued for divorce on the grounds that his wife had hidden her mixed-race origins from him. During the trial, Jones's attorney had requested that she strip to the waist as proof that her husband had clearly known all along that she was black.

Because the court had barred photographers from witnessing this display, the *Evening Graphic* staged a composograph of Jones displaying her nude torso to the all-white jury. It was made by combining separate photographs of all the people involved and resizing them to proportion. Harry Grogin, the assistant art director, also arranged for an actress to be photographed semi naked in a pose that he imagined Alice would have taken. Grogin is said to have used 20 separate photos to arrive at the one compiled shot, but the resulting picture was believable. The *Evening Graphic*'s circulation rose from 60,000 to several hundred thousand after that issue.

Despite healthy sales, the paper struggled financially because its trashy reputation did not attract advertisers. In spite of the financial position, Macfadden continued to plough his own money into the venture. The paper lasted just eight years – from 1924 to 1932 – and Macfadden is said to have lost over USD$10 million in the process. But the sensationalism, nudity and inventive methods of reporting set a model for tabloid journalism as we know it today.

Is producing fake images of real situations unethical?

Is it unethical to produce images based on sensationalism and nudity?

Would you have created composographs for the *Evening Graphic*?

A photograph is a secret about a secret. The more it tells you the less you know.

Diane Arbus

Working with ethics

Further reading

AIGA
Design Business and Ethics
2007, AIGA

Eaton, Marcia Muelder
Aesthetics and the Good Life
1989, Associated University Press

Ellison, David
Ethics and Aesthetics in European Modernist Literature:
From the Sublime to the Uncanny
2001, Cambridge University Press

Fenner, David E W (Ed)
Ethics and the Arts:
An Anthology
1995, Garland Reference Library of Social Science

Gini, Al and Marcoux, Alexei M
Case Studies in Business Ethics
2005, Prentice Hall

McDonough, William and Braungart, Michael
Cradle to Cradle:
Remaking the Way We Make Things
2002, North Point Press

Papanek, Victor
Design for the Real World:
Making to Measure
1972, Thames & Hudson

United Nations Global Compact
The Ten Principles
www.unglobalcompact.org/AboutTheGC/TheTenPrinciples/index.html